GOOD HOUSEKEEPING
Low-Calorie BIG-FLAVOR COOKBOOK

This book is intended as a reference volume only, not as a medical manual. The information given here is designed to help you make informed decisions about your health. It is not intended as a substitute for any treatment that may have been prescribed by your doctor. If you suspect that you have a medical problem, we urge you to seek competent medical help.

© 2022 by Hearst Magazine Media, Inc.

All rights reserved. No part of this publication may be reproduced or transmitted in any form or by any means, electronic or mechanical, including photocopying, recording, or any other information storage and retrieval system, without the written permission of the publisher.

Good Housekeeping is a registered trademark of Hearst Communications, Inc.

Cover Photography
Danielle Daly

Interior Photography
Mike Garten: 8, 22, 25-41, 47, 49, 55, 63-71, 75, 79-103, 107-138, 143-153, 157-179, 183-201, 213-259, 265-290, 293-325; Getty Images: fcafotodigital/E+: 12; Iryna Melnyk/Moment: 18; Claudia Totir/Moment: 21; Westend61: 10; Danielle Daly: 43, 51, 53, 57, 60, 77, 105, 133, 155, 181, 189, 203-211, 261-263, 327; Con Poulos: 45, 59, 141; Christopher Testani: 4, 73, Sarah Anne Ward: 269

Book design by Izzy Lamb

Recipes by Anna Helm Baxter, Ayesha Curry, Gabriella Vigoreaux, Good Housekeeping Test Kitchen, Kate Merker, Khalil Hymore, Taylor Murray, Kristina Kurek, Prevention Test Kitchen, Sandy Carmo, Woman's Day Kitchen

Library of Congress Cataloging-in-Publication Data is on file with the publisher.

ISBN 978-1-950099-93-1

Printed in China

2 4 6 8 10 9 7 5 3 1 paperback

HEARST

GOOD HOUSEKEEPING
Low-Calorie BIG-FLAVOR COOKBOOK

Hot Pepper & Onion Pizza
p. 73

table of CONTENTS

INTRODUCTION 9

Breakfast 22

Greek Yogurt Pancakes 25
Blueberry Muffins 27
Raspberry Chia Jam 29
Pineapple Cucumber Smoothie 31
Peach Mango Smoothie 33
Winter Citrus Fruit Salad 35
Blueberry-Banana-Nut Smoothie 37
Super-Simple Summer Smoothie 39
Shakshuka 41

Breakfast Tacos 43
Almond-Berry French Toast Bake 45
Very Berry Quinoa Muffins 47
Easiest Ever Bagels 49
Mason Jar Scramble 51
Pear & Cottage Cheese Toast 53
Spiced Plum & Quinoa Muffins 55
Spinach & Goat Cheese Egg Muffins 57
Fruit & Nut Bars 59

Lunch 60

Butternut Squash & Spinach Toasts 63
Charred Scallion Tart 65
Spring Panzanella 67
Roasted Butternut Squash Salad
  with Tahini Vinaigrette 69
Quinoa-Stuffed Acorn Squash
  with Cranberries & Feta 71
Hot Pepper & Onion Pizza 73
Vegetable Torte 75
White Bean & Tuna Salad
  with Basil Vinaigrette 77

Seared Coconut-Lime Chicken
  with Snap Pea Slaw 79
Grilled Eggplant with Chickpea Croutons 81
Grilled Green Beans, Fennel & Farro 83
Peach & Prosciutto Flatbreads 85
Tuscan-Style Tomato & Bread Salad 87
Chicken Soup with Spinach & Lemon 89
Charred Shrimp, Leek &
  Asparagus Skewers 91
Rhubarb & Citrus Salad
  with Black Pepper Vinaigrette 93

Cauliflower Fried Rice **95**
Shrimp Ceviche **97**
Peach Caprese Salad **99**
Warm Roasted Cauliflower
   & Spinach Salad **101**
Spice-Dusted Pork with
   Crunchy Vegetable Salad **103**
Blackened Fish Tacos **105**
Barley Salad with Strawberries &
   Buttermilk Dressing **107**
Korean Pineapple Beef Lettuce Wraps **109**
Roasted Asparagus & Ricotta Tart **111**
Grilled Lamb & Artichoke Kebabs **113**

Savory Stone Fruit Soup **115**
White Bean & Kale Toasts **117**
Roasted Red Pepper Soup **119**
Broccoli "Steaks" with Spicy Tomato Jam **121**
Cucumber-Melon Soup **123**
Chilled Corn Soup **125**
Tomato Soup with Parmesan Crostini **127**
Caribbean-Style Fish with Peppers **129**
Jerk Shrimp Wraps with Mango Slaw **131**
Sheet Pan Chicken Fajitas **133**
Chicken & Avocado Salad Arepas **135**
Chicken Roulades with
   Marinated Tomatoes **137**

Dinner **138**

Seafood, Chorizo & Vegetable Stew **141**
Mushroom & Brussels Sprouts Pizza **143**
Sheet Pan Sausage & Egg Breakfast Bake **145**
Shrimp Curry & Rice **147**
Orecchiette with White Beans & Spinach **149**
Chicken with Sautéed Apples
   & Mushrooms **151**
Orange-Ginger Roast Chicken with Fennel
   & Radicchio Salad **153**
Rotisserie Chicken Cobb Salad **155**
Pulled Pork Nachos **157**
Chicken Mole **159**
Greek Lemon Chicken Soup **161**
Roast Lamb **163**
Beef & Broccoli **165**
Summer Squash Pizza **167**
Marinated Flank Steak
   with Grilled Broccoli **169**
Shrimp Enchiladas With Zucchini & Corn **171**
Grilled Fajita Kebabs **173**
Oven-Roasted Salmon with Charred
   Lemon Vinaigrette **175**

Cod in Parchment with Orange-
   and-Leek Couscous **177**
Bánh Mì **179**
Crispy Chicken Thighs with Buttermilk
   Fennel Salad **181**
Spring Vegetable Pizza **183**
Pea Fritters with Shrimp Salad **185**
Lemon-Thyme Chicken **187**
Spiced Cod with Rice Noodle Salad **189**
Light Chicken Cacciatore **191**
Five-Spice Beef Stew **193**
Sausage Cauliflower Cassoulet **195**
Tomato-Basil Gnocchi **197**
Mixed Greens & Herb Toss Salad **199**
Herbed Ricotta & Fresh Tomato Tart **201**
Roasted Salmon with
   Green Beans & Tomatoes **203**
White Bean Cassoulet
   with Pork & Lentils **205**
Grilled Pork with Charred
   Harissa Broccoli **207**
Vegetable Ramen with
   Mushrooms and Bok Choy **209**

Shrimp Boil with Sausage and Spinach 211
Wild Mushroom Toasts 213
Enchiladas Verdes 215
Fiery Black Bean Soup 217
Creamy Corn Chowder 219
Charred Shrimp & Avocado Salad 221
Shrimp Rolls 223
Wild Mushroom Risotto 225
Coconut Curry Chicken 227
Mini Meatballs with Garlicky Tomatoes 229
Oil & Vinegar Chicken Cutlet Sandwiches 231
Pan-Fried Chicken with Lemony
    Roasted Broccoli 233
Cheesy Chicken & Broccoli Casserole 235
Classic Omelet & Greens 237

Beef Kofte with Kale & Chickpea Salad 239
Hearty Bean and Beef Chili 241
Paprika Chicken with Crispy Chickpeas
    & Tomatoes 243
Grilled Chicken Skewers & Kale Caesar 245
Chicken and Broccoli Parchment Packets 247
Striped Bass with Radish Salsa Verde 249
Spring Herb Frittata 251
Fennel Pasta Pomodoro 253
Savory Lentil Waffles 255
Soy-Glazed Meatloaf 257
Slow Cooker BBQ Jackfruit Sandwich
    with Pineapple Slaw 259
Speedy Eggplant Parmesan 261

Dessert 262

Mini Chocolate Chip Sandwiches 265
Eggnog Truffles 267
Flourless Chocolate Walnut Cookies 269
Pecan Sticky Buns 271
Meyer Lemon Madeleines 273
Pecan Berry Bursts 275
Fudgy Beet Brownies 277

Italian Shaved Ice Granita 279
Pumpkin Spice Mousse 281
White Chocolate & Lavender Madeleines 283
No-Churn Mango Berry Ice Cream 285
Vanilla Bean Clafoutis with
    Raspberries & Nectarines 287
Clementine Honey Granita 289

Snacks 290

Dill Dip 293
Chickpea "Nuts" 295
Roasted Strawberries & Brie 297
Spinach & Yogurt Dip 299
Muhammara Dip 301
Yellow Split Pea Dip 303
Fried Plantains 305
Spring Crudités with Herbed Cheese Dip 307
Zesty Beet Dip 309

Best Ever Spinach-Artichoke Dip 311
Zucchanoush 313
Charred Salsa 315
Prosciutto Scallion Bundles 317
Roasted Artichokes with Caesar Dip 319
Garlicky Roasted-Radish Bruschetta 321
Spinach Artichoke Tartines 323
Raspberry Popcorn 325
Sweet & Salty Maple Popcorn 327

Chicken with Sautéed Apples & Mushrooms

p. 151

Introduction

When it comes to losing weight, there are few approaches as uncomplicated as low-calorie eating. The basic rule? Consume fewer calories than you burn. But so many plans based on this rule have a reputation for being bland, boring and impossible to stick with. And that's led a lot of people to think that cutting calories means cutting flavor and limiting your plate to steamed veggies and unseasoned chicken breast.

But there's good news. In the Good Housekeeping Test Kitchen, we've been creating delicious, nutritious recipes for more than a century, so we knew there had to be a way to bring that same balance of great flavor and healthy foods to low-calorie cooking. After all, what good is a low-calorie dish if it leaves you craving more?

When tackling this challenge, we knew each recipe needed to contain three things: the most nourishing low-calorie ingredients to give you more bang for your bite, hunger-fighting protein and fiber and, of course, as much flavor as possible. The 150+ tried-and-tested recipes that make up this book are all of those things and more. And here, you'll find something for everyone — delicious 20-minute meals, family favorites, slow-cooker dinners that simmer for hours, plus snacks (the spinach artichoke dip on page 311 is a must-try) and desserts (there is ice cream on page 285—yes, ice cream!). Every meal clocks in at 500 calories or less per serving and includes complete nutritional information, so you can easily integrate these recipes into your daily meal plan, whatever your nutrition goals may be.

Whether you are in search of a new main, a lighter treat to serve family and friends, or just looking to change up your dinnertime routine, we hope these recipes show you that healthy eating can be satisfying — and most of all, full of flavor.

Happy cooking (and eating),

KATE MERKER
Chief Food Director, Good Housekeeping

STEFANI SASSOS, MS, RDN, CDN
Registered Dietitian, Good Housekeeping Institute

the BASICS

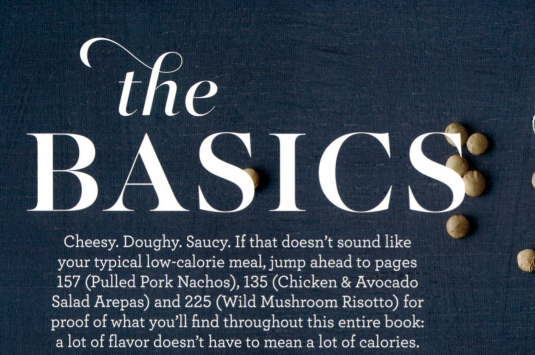

Cheesy. Doughy. Saucy. If that doesn't sound like your typical low-calorie meal, jump ahead to pages 157 (Pulled Pork Nachos), 135 (Chicken & Avocado Salad Arepas) and 225 (Wild Mushroom Risotto) for proof of what you'll find throughout this entire book: a lot of flavor doesn't have to mean a lot of calories.

When done the smart way, low-calorie eating can include a variety of cuisines, foods, tastes and textures. It can even include cookies and brownies. The secret is to use the right ingredients in the right amounts, which is exactly what the experts at the Good Housekeeping Test Kitchen have done for every recipe here. Each dish has been triple-tested to make sure it will leave you feeling satisfied, nourished and happy.

When you approach this way of eating with fun, flavorful and filling meals, a low-calorie lifestyle may be easier to maintain. This weight-loss method relies on a simple principle: consume fewer calories than you burn each day. But what makes it a bit more sustainable is that in order to actually eat fewer calories overall, you have to eat more of the right calories. The right calories come from nutrient-dense, fiber-filled foods that are high in antioxidants, water and key minerals that help you stay satisfied and energized. A low-calorie diet usually entails consuming between 1,200 and 1,500 calories per day in order to achieve long-term weight loss. Every recipe here is under 500 calories, so you can easily find breakfasts, lunches, dinners and even desserts that fit into your daily calorie goals.

Unlike many other diets, which require cutting out certain foods completely, a low-calorie plan allows you to eat essentially whatever you want as long as it falls within your daily calorie allowance. However, the secret to creating a way of eating you can adhere to in the long run lies in picking the foods that will fill you up and keep you motivated—and avoiding those that will leave you feeling deprived and less likely to stick to the program. Instead, pick big-flavor foods that will fill you up and keep you motivated.

INTRODUCTION **11**

The Best Low-Calorie Foods

As a general rule, stick to whole foods and avoid consuming a lot of processed foods and sugar. To identify better choices for low-calorie foods that will keep you feeling full for longer, look for those that offer generous amounts of protein and fiber. Both work to fill you up and support other vital functions.

PROTEIN

This mighty macronutrient helps to keep your blood sugar stable, preventing highs and lows throughout the day (meaning you won't end up with a growling stomach one hour after breakfast). Nearly everything in our bodies requires protein, including our skin, blood and bones. It's key for cell tissue repair and regeneration. And since protein takes longer to digest than carbs, protein-rich meals can also keep you fuller, longer.

Lean protein is a key component in any well-balanced diet. Ideally you should include it in every meal and snack. On a low-calorie diet, good sources of lean protein include chicken (without the skin), eggs, dairy, seafood, lean cuts of red meat, tofu and legumes. For the average person, eating 1 gram of protein per kilogram of body weight per day is ideal. If you're physically active, you may need more protein.

FIBER

Fiber slows gut transit time so that it takes you longer to digest what you ate. It's found in a variety of plant-based foods, including fruits, vegetables, grains, legumes, nuts and seeds. It helps to keep your digestive tract moving properly, aids in weight management and helps to remove extra circulating cholesterol, all while building good gut bacteria. The daily recommended allowance for women is 21-25 grams; for men, it's 30-38 grams. The key to increasing fiber in your diet is to start slowly to avoid bloating, constipation and/or gassiness, and to make sure you're well hydrated to keep things moving.

Pure fiber itself has virtually no calories. Your body can't break it down, so it runs right through your digestive system, providing only bulk. It's important to know that although the distinction isn't always apparent in food labels, there are two types of fiber: insoluble and soluble. Most fiber-rich foods contain both types — the insoluble kind helps improve your digestion, and the soluble kind gives fiber its disease-fighting clout. Soluble fiber, in particular, helps whittle your waist.

High-fiber foods take a long time to chew, giving your body time to send "I'm full" signals to the brain before you've overeaten. These foods also tend to take up space in your stomach, so you're likely to stay full for longer periods of time.

The Low-Calorie KITCHEN

You're more likely to stay the course on any diet when your kitchen is well stocked with healthy ingredients. The items below are all low in calories and full of flavor. Many of these staples can be purchased frozen as well, so they'll stay fresh well after the week you buy them. Keep a supply of your favorites on hand and you'll always be minutes away from something delicious and nourishing.

PRODUCE

APPLES: They deliver around 100 calories and 4 grams of fiber per serving, which makes them one of the best fruits for weight loss.

ARUGULA: Like spinach and other leafy greens, arugula lets you go big on the serving size for very few calories. There's just 25 calories in 5 whole cups.

ASPARAGUS: At just 27 calories per cup, the veggie makes for one super low-cal side dish. As an added bonus, asparagus is rich in insoluble fiber, which research suggests can thwart the release of hunger hormones and help keep your blood sugar stable.

BROCCOLI: Not only is this one of the most versatile vegetables, it's a great source of vitamin C and fiber. Broccoli can be enjoyed raw, steamed, sautéed, grilled, roasted...the possibilities are endless.

CABBAGE: We don't recommend trying to subsist solely on cabbage soup. But the veggie is crazy low in calories — with just 18 in a cup of shredded cabbage. Use it to bulk up stir-fries, stews or salads.

CANTALOUPE: An entire cup of cubed cantaloupe is just 56 calories, so it's the perfect snack when you're craving something sweet.

CAULIFLOWER: Similar to broccoli, although with a lighter, milder flavor, cauliflower can also be enjoyed steamed, riced, roasted, grilled — you can even make pizza crust out of it. It's also full of vitamin C and fiber, and it's loaded with antioxidants.

CELERY: At around 5 calories per stalk, celery is one of nature's lowest-cal foods. Its fiber is key for slowing digestion and helps you feel fuller, longer.

CUCUMBER: Try cuke slices as dippers in place of starchy crackers. An entire large cucumber has just 28 calories, but a measly handful of crackers will cost you 150.

RADISHES: Craving a crunchy snack? You could have a handful of potato chips for around 150 calories...or an entire cup of sliced radishes topped with sea salt for just 19 calories.

RASPBERRIES: All berries are packed with antioxidant polyphenols and vitamins, but raspberries really reign supreme in the fiber department. A cup of raspberries has only 64 calories but boasts a whopping 8 grams of fiber, so they make a perfect low-calorie but nutrient-dense snack.

SNOW PEAS: There are only 30 calories in half a cup of the crisp green pods.

SPINACH: Don't be shy about piling on these leafy greens the next time you have a salad or sandwich. You'd have to eat 15 cups of spinach to even crack the 100-calorie mark. So they're a smart way to add filling volume to your meals.

ZUCCHINI AND YELLOW SQUASH: Each cup has just 19 calories — and loads of culinary potential.

MEATS/FISH

BONELESS, SKINLESS CHICKEN BREAST: It's a weight-loss staple food for a reason. A 3-oz serving of boneless, skinless chicken breast has only 102 calories — but nearly 20 grams of protein.

FLOUNDER: A 3-oz serving of flounder has only 73 calories, making it one of the lowest-calorie fish out there.

PORK TENDERLOIN: Low-cal might not be the first thing that comes to mind when you think of pork. But cuts like pork tenderloin are actually super lean: A 3-oz serving has just 122 calories.

SCALLOPS: They might taste indulgent, but 5 small scallops have only 25 calories. Just don't undo the goodness by drowning them in butter or wrapping them in bacon.

SHRIMP: At 84 calories for 3 oz, the tiny swimmers are a waistline-friendly protein option. (You'll get 20 grams of the muscle builder per serving.)

DRY GOODS

BLACK BEANS: At 114 calories per half cup when cooked, these are one of the lowest-calorie beans you can eat. They're also loaded with protein and fiber.

CHICKPEA PASTA: If you're looking for more protein and fiber but fewer carbs than regular pasta, look no further. This is a great way to add more nutrition, vitamins and minerals to your favorite comfort food dish.

GREEN TEA: Not only is it calorie-free (when you skip the added sugar or milk, of course), but it also has antioxidant benefits. Green tea is rich in epigallocatechin gallate (EGCG), which has been shown to work in tandem with caffeine to promote fat burning.

LENTILS: A half cup of cooked lentils has 12 grams of protein for just 140 calories. The super-versatile legume can be added to grain bowls, salads, soups and more.

NUTS: All nuts are loaded with fiber, but almonds in particular have about 3.5 grams of fiber per ounce, which is more than most nuts. Slivered almonds taste great on top of oatmeal or yogurt, and we love them toasted as a garnish on roasted green beans or asparagus.

OATS/OATMEAL: Swap it for a bakery-style muffin at breakfast, and you could save hundreds of calories. A cup of oatmeal cooked in water has just 150 calories. Oats and oatmeal have their fiber content to thank for the slew of health benefits they provide, including improving heart health, balancing your blood sugar, and helping you manage your weight. Just half a cup of dry oats contains 4 grams of dietary fiber.

POPCORN: Believe it or not, popcorn is considered a whole grain and is a good source of fiber. Skip the movie theater popcorn dripping in butter, and opt for air-popped or light oil-popped varieties. Pre-portioned packs are always a good idea, or you can buy a big bag of popcorn and portion it out yourself into individual baggies to have for the week.

PUMPKIN PUREE: Use it in place of butter to lighten up muffins, quickbreads or even brownies in a big way.

REFRIGERATED

EGGS: A large egg packs 6 grams of belly-filling protein for 70 calories. And they won't squash your appetite only while you're eating them. Research shows that eggs can curb your calorie intake at your next meal too.

HUMMUS: Thanks to its main ingredient, chickpeas, this delicious spread makes a good source of dietary fiber and plant-based protein. Plus, hummus is packed with several vitamins and minerals such as folate, calcium, magnesium and potassium.

LOW-FAT COTTAGE CHEESE: It's got about one-fifth of the calories you'll find in most cheeses. Plus, it's higher in protein, serving up around 28 grams per cup. That can help keep your appetite in check for longer — and keep your metabolism revved.

NONFAT MILK: It might be a drink instead of food, but don't discount it. All that liquid takes up lots of room in your stomach, and an 8-oz glass boasts 8 grams of protein for only 86 calories. Bottoms up!

Foods to *Limit*

No single food in isolation of everything else you eat is going to make you gain (or lose!) weight. But often, the same barrier stumps so many people when it comes to weight loss and healthier eating: sneaky sources of added sugar or saturated fat lurking throughout the pantry, fridge or freezer.

Many times these foods are marketed as healthier options, leading you to buy them for their purported benefits — but actually, you might've been much more satisfied if you'd chosen the real thing instead. Other times, these foods have replaced the calories coming from one type of nutrient with another. For example, keto snacks swap sugar for high-fat coconut oil or butter; low-fat foods swap fat for added sugar. Read labels carefully — especially anything with a "free," "low" or "less" claim — to make sure you're making a choice that works best for you.

OUR BEST TIP

Prioritize real, wholesome foods in their closest-to-natural state as often as possible. (The only ingredient in your peanut butter should be peanuts!) The fewer the ingredients, generally the better it is for you. This helps you get super picky about what you're really in the mood to eat, while helping you determine what choices will maximize your enjoyment and minimize self-sabotage. To the right are some examples of sneaky foods that actually make you gain weight.

"HEALTHY" FOODS THAT AREN'T REALLY THAT HEALTHY

CEREAL: Cereals are deceptive for two reasons: First, many are secret sugar bombs, especially if you aren't sticking to the suggested serving size. Second, because sugary cereals are sometimes low in fiber, they can leave you ravenous when lunch is hours away.

COCONUT OIL: Coconut oil was never the elixir it was touted to be, with one tablespoon packing 117 calories, 14 grams total fat and 12 grams saturated fat (60% of the daily value). The bottom line is that having a tablespoon a day is unlikely to harm anyone, but there's no data to support coconut oil as a cure-all.

AGAVE NECTAR: Your body processes sweeteners like agave nectar, honey, maple syrup, evaporated cane juice and corn syrup pretty much the same way as it does plain old white or brown sugar — so you should watch how much you eat or drink no matter which type is used. Like regular sugar, agave syrup contains about 45–60 calories per tablespoon.

BOTTLED SMOOTHIES AND JUICES: Fruit smoothies and juices are often just extra-sugary versions of previously good-for-you foods. Look for blended beverages under 12 grams of sugar a pop to ensure that your snack contains more protein than sweet stuff. It'll help you stay satisfied and keep cravings at bay.

PROTEIN SHAKES: Protein shakes do have a place in life (like if you're having trouble chewing), but most of us add them to our day instead of swapping them in. Most hover between 250–600 calories per 16-oz serving, making them a hearty snack for some and a mini-meal for others. Check labels on any protein powder to make sure you're choosing ones with minimal added sugar. And if you're drinking them as post-workout fuel, you may be better off with a piece of fruit and cheese to tide you over until meal time.

GRANOLA BARS: Some are better than others, but our biggest gripe with breakfast bars is their promise of being "satisfying." With too little protein, fiber and fat, many simply won't fill you up. Look for those that provide at least 4 grams each of protein and fiber, and less than 6 grams of added sugar per serving. The first ingredient should be an actual food (e.g., almonds, dates, apples); skip bars that contain a protein isolate. If you choose a granola bar, add nuts, nut butter, hard-boiled eggs or an unsweetened low-fat latte to your breakfast for a better nutritional profile.

NON-DAIRY CHEESE: This is another example where you might assume the alternative version has fewer calories than the original — but it doesn't. Vegan cheese still has about 100 calories per ounce, just like the regular kind, and it's loaded with fake ingredients such as starch, xanthan gum and protein isolates. Additionally, you're losing the protein-rich benefit of the real deal: String cheese has 6 grams of protein, whereas a serving of vegan cheese contains about 0.3 gram — so you won't even feel as full from each serving.

FRUIT JUICE: Essentially a concentrated source of sugar and calories, fruit juice is void of any fiber and eliminates most of the nutritional benefits of eating the fruit in its whole form. A piece of whole fruit is always better than a cup of juice, but sometimes you just want to sip a refreshing drink. Try slicing a few pieces of fruit and letting them infuse in your water. Not only does it add a great burst of flavor, but it'll also contribute to your hydration for the day.

YOGURT-COVERED SNACKS: Although you may think you're making a healthy choice by choosing yogurt-covered pretzels and raisins, these actually tend to contain more sugar than even chocolate-coated options. Grab a portion-controlled handful of pretzels or a few pieces of fruit and dip them into yogurt for a far less sugary option than the yogurt candy variety.

FLAVORED YOGURT: While we're talking about yogurt, you should know that not all yogurt is healthy. Check the ingredients label to make sure it's full of words you know and can pronounce. More importantly, take a look at the sugar content. A standard 6-oz yogurt container shouldn't have more than 10 grams of added sugar. Opt for plain yogurt and flavor it yourself using nature's candy (a.k.a. fruit). Load it up with berries for tons of fiber and antioxidants. Bonus points for picking Greek yogurt, which has a ton of filling protein.

DRIED FRUIT: Of course dried fruit is still full of nutrients, but it can be much higher in sugar than fresh fruit. Plus, certain varieties, like cranberries, are often dried with sugar added to them so they taste super sweet. Nature's candy is always king and makes a perfect snack any time of day. Plus, it's excellent in a bowl of oatmeal to tide you over for the afternoon. Instead of dried fruit, try adding fresh blueberries to trail mix for a refreshing twist!

In addition to these foods, aim to limit anything processed. These foods usually include a lot of fat, sugar and salt, which are used to increase flavor and extend shelf life. They can also contain less fiber. Replacing sugary beverages and soda with water, avoiding processed meats and consuming fresh or frozen fruits and veggies instead of packaged and processed foods are a few ways to avoid processed ingredients.

When following any diet and especially a low-calorie diet, it is best to keep all sugar to a minimum because sugar drives hunger. Aim for less than 24 grams of added sugar per day for women and less than 36 grams for men. Look out for added sugars, which could be listed (hidden) as a number of different items on the label including agave, brown sugar, honey, maple syrup, molasses, corn syrup, brown rice syrup or and/or anything that ends in "ose" (as in fructose, sucrose and others).

Low-Calorie Ingredient Swaps

An easy way to jump-start a low-calorie diet is by swapping high-calorie foods for low-calorie ones. This will help you create a deficit that leads to weight loss. It's also a great way to sneak in more veggies because they are naturally low calorie, and many can stand in for higher-fat ingredients. The foods below all mimic their high-calorie counterparts in some way (taste, texture, etc.), giving you all the flavor without all the calories.

LOW-CALORIE INGREDIENT SWAPS

High-Calorie Ingredient	Low-Calorie Swap
Mayonnaise	Avocado or Hummus
Butter	Pumpkin Puree or Olive Oil
Bread or Tortilla	Romaine Lettuce
Croutons	Walnuts
Mashed Potatoes	Mashed Cauliflower
Bagel	English Muffin
Spaghetti	Spaghetti Squash

LOW-CALORIE RESTAURANT SWAPS

High-Calorie Ingredient	Low-Calorie Swap
Sour Cream	Low-Fat Greek Yogurt
Salad Dressing	Olive Oil, Vinegar, Lemon
Hamburger Bun	Lettuce or Collard Green Wrap
Rice	Cauliflower Rice
Tortilla Chips	Veggies
Soda, Alcohol	Seltzer with Fruit Slices, Mint
Pizza Crust	Tortilla or Cauliflower Crust

LOW-CALORIE, BIG-FLAVOR

(ALMOST) ZERO-CALORIE FLAVOR BOOSTERS

A good-quality sauce or condiment is a simple yet delicious way to add a true flavor boost to any meal. But most brands on the market are loaded with excessive amounts of sodium, added sugar, artificial sweeteners and other not-so-great ingredients. If you're looking to make some healthy changes to your diet but don't want to sacrifice flavor, there are still a variety of ways you can enjoy your meals without piling on the calories.

HERBS & SPICES

There's simply no better way to add delicious, complex flavors to your meals — with essentially no extra calories, salt, sugar or fat.

- **OREGANO**
- **GARLIC POWDER**
- **TURMERIC**
- **CINNAMON**
- **BASIL**
- **CILANTRO**
- **ROSEMARY**

SAUCES & CONDIMENTS

Store-bought sauces are a quick and easy way to infuse more flavor into a meal, but be careful of added sugar and sodium.

- **APPLE CIDER VINEGAR**
- **BALSAMIC VINEGAR**
- **MUSTARD**
- **HOT SAUCE**

FLAVOR EXTRACTS

Vanilla extract has 0 calories and sugars (compared to the 80 calories and 20 grams of sugar in a serving of vanilla syrup flavoring). Start with one drop and add to taste; a little goes a long way.

- **VANILLA EXTRACT**
- **PEPPERMINT EXTRACT**
- **ALMOND EXTRACT**

LOW-CALORIE FLAVOR COMBOS

Pick a hearty base then add these delicious seasonings and condiments to inject major flavor minus the calories.

SEAFOOD
- Salmon + Fresh Basil + Lemon
- Salmon + Herbes de Provence + Dijon Mustard + Red Wine Vinegar + Garlic + Lemon Zest
- Cod + Lime + Cilantro + Chipotle Chili Powder + Red Onion

MEAT
- Chicken Breast + Tomatoes + Garlic + Oregano
- Chicken Breast + Hot Sauce + Low-Fat Greek Yogurt + Green Onions
- Pork Loin + Balsamic + Rosemary

VEGETARIAN
- Cauliflower + Tahini + Turmeric + Cilantro + Red Pepper Flakes
- Tofu/Tempeh + Coconut Aminos + Hot Sauce + Garlic + Ginger

Tips for Cutting Calories

When it comes to all things weight loss, the simplest, fastest way to make impactful, lasting change is to form habits you can actually stick with for life. Here are a few tips that you can put into practice right now to start cutting down on calories.

LOAD UP ON VEGGIES.
If you think about making any meal mostly veggies (at least 50% of anything that you're having), you're on the right track to better health.

BUILD A BETTER BREAKFAST.
All meals are important, but a healthy breakfast will help you start your day right. The best, heartiest breakfasts will fill you up, keep you satisfied and stave off cravings later in the day. Aim to eat anywhere between 400 and 500 calories for your morning meal, and make sure you're including a source of lean protein plus filling fat (e.g., eggs, unsweetened Greek yogurt, nuts or nut butters) and fiber (veggies, fruit or 100% whole grains). Starting your day with a blood sugar-stabilizing blend of nutrients will help you slim down.

SKIP SUGARY BEVERAGES.
Drinking a juice or caramel coffee drink just isn't as satisfying as eating a bowl of veggie- or protein-packed stir-fry. So monitor your intake of juice, soda, sweetened coffee and tea, and alcoholic beverages. If you consume each of those beverages during the day, you'll have taken in at least 800 extra calories by night — and you'll still be hungry.

EAT SPICY FOODS — SERIOUSLY!
It can actually help you cut back on calories. That's because capsaicin, a compound found in jalapeño and cayenne peppers, may (slightly) increase your body's release of stress hormones such as adrenaline, which can speed up your ability to burn calories. What's more, eating hot peppers may help you eat more slowly and avoid overeating. You're more likely to stay mindful about when you're full. Some great choices besides hot peppers: ginger and turmeric.

RESIST THE URGE TO SKIP A MEAL.
Going long periods without food does double-duty harm to your healthy-eating efforts by both slowing down your metabolism and priming you for a binge later in the day. (Think: You've skipped breakfast and lunch, so you're ready to take down a whole turkey by dinner!) Make it your mission to eat three meals and two snacks every day, and don't go longer than three to four hours without eating. Set a "snack alarm" on your phone if needed.

SNACK IN THE AFTERNOON INSTEAD OF THE MORNING.
If you're divvying up your total daily calories across five or six smaller meals in order to control hunger and lose weight, you may be able to get by with one less snack and slim down even more. According to a study published in the *Journal of the American Dietetic Association*, a mid-morning snack is less effective for weight loss than a mid-afternoon one. Researchers speculate the finding may have less to do with when we snack than the simple fact that there's not as much time between breakfast and lunch for most people as there is between lunch and dinner. Thus, morning snackers may be guilty of mindless eating and probably could forgo that feeding without getting ravenous and overeating at lunch.

RECIPE REFERENCE ICONS

Look for these icons throughout the book to identify recipes for different nutrition needs.

HIGH FIBER
Contains more than 5 grams of fiber per serving.

HIGH PROTEIN
Contains more than 20 grams of protein per serving.

VEGETARIAN
Does not contain meat, poultry or seafood.

GLUTEN-FREE
Does not contain gluten, a protein found in wheat.

LOW-CARB
Contains 30 grams or less of carbohydrates per serving.

DAIRY-FREE
Does not contain dairy products, including cheese, milk and butter.

Raspberry Chia Jam
p. 29

Chapter One
Breakfast

Breakfast

Greek Yogurt Pancakes

Add a protein boost to your favorite breakfast with these fluffy and nourishing pancakes made with yogurt. Make a double batch on Saturday morning and freeze leftovers for a quick morning meal later in the week.

PER SERVING
~225 cal, 4 g fat (2 g sat), 9 g protein, 480 mg sodium, 36 g carb, 1 g fiber

ACTIVE TIME 25 min. **TOTAL TIME** 25 min. **YIELDS** 4 servings

INGREDIENTS

- ½ cup vanilla Greek yogurt
- 2 large eggs
- ⅓ cup milk
- 2 Tbsp maple syrup
- 1 tsp pure vanilla extract
- 1 cup all-purpose flour
- ¾ tsp baking soda
- ½ tsp baking powder
- ¼ tsp kosher salt
- Yogurt, strawberries, blueberries and syrup, for topping

DIRECTIONS

1. In large bowl, whisk together yogurt, eggs, milk, syrup and vanilla.

2. In second bowl, whisk together flour, baking soda, baking powder and salt.

3. Add flour mixture to yogurt mixture and mix to combine (batter should be like thick papier-mâché).

4. Heat large nonstick skillet on medium (see tip below). Check heat by sprinkling pan with water—when water bubbles and evaporates immediately, it's ready.

5. Spoon about 2 Tbsp batter per pancake on pan, or 1 Tbsp for smaller pancakes. Cook pancakes until bubbles begin to appear around edges and in centers. Using spatula, peek under pancakes to check that they are golden brown, then carefully flip. Cook about 1 min. more depending on size. Transfer to wire rack and cover loosely with foil to keep warm or serve immediately, topped with yogurt, strawberries, blueberries and syrup.

TIP

If your nonstick skillet is past its prime and pancakes stick, add 1 tsp canola or vegetable oil and heat it before pouring next batch.

CHAPTER ONE: BREAKFAST

Breakfast

Blueberry Muffins

Heaps of fresh blueberries and a sprinkle of sugar give this grab-and-go breakfast bursts of berries inside and a crackly top—and at just 250 calories a muffin.

PER SERVING
~250 cal, 9.5 g fat (5.5 g sat), 4 g pro, 375 mg sodium, 39 g carb, 1 g fiber

ACTIVE TIME 50 min. **TOTAL TIME** 10 min. **YIELDS** 12 servings

INGREDIENTS

- 2 cups blueberries, divided
- 1¾ cups plus 2 tsp all-purpose flour
- 2¼ tsp baking powder
- 1½ tsp kosher salt
- ¼ tsp freshly grated nutmeg
- 1 stick unsalted butter, at room temp
- 1 cup granulated sugar
- 1 large egg plus 1 large egg yolk, at room temp
- 1½ tsp vanilla extract
- 1 cup buttermilk
- 2 Tbsp turbinado sugar (we used Sugar in the Raw)

DIRECTIONS

1. Heat oven to 425°F. Cut 12 5-in. parchment paper squares. Line each cup of 12-cup muffin pan with parchment square, pressing down with a drinking glass to form cup shape and flattening folds. Set aside ½ cup blueberries; toss remaining 1½ cups blueberries with 2 tsp flour.

2. In medium bowl, whisk together remaining 1¾ cups flour, baking powder, salt and nutmeg.

3. In large bowl with electric mixer, beat butter and granulated sugar on medium-high speed until light and fluffy, 3 to 4 min. Reduce mixer speed to medium and add whole egg and yolk in 2 additions, beating after each until incorporated before adding the next and scraping down bowl as necessary. Beat in vanilla.

4. Reduce mixer speed to low and add flour mixture in three parts, alternating with buttermilk and beating just until incorporated, scraping bowl as necessary. Do not overmix. Fold in floured blueberries, leaving behind any excess flour that does not cling to berries.

5. Divide batter among muffin cups (about a heaping ⅓ cup each). Cups will seem very full. Sprinkle with turbinado sugar and press remaining ½ cup blueberries into tops of muffins. Bake on middle rack until wooden pick inserted in center comes out with a few loose crumbs attached, 20 to 22 min. Let cool in pan 5 min., then transfer to wire rack to cool completely.

Breakfast

Raspberry Chia Jam

Chia seeds are a great source of fiber, minerals and plant-based omega-3 fatty acids, making this a nutritious, lower-calorie alternative to your average jar of jelly.

PER SERVING
~20 cal,
0.5 g fat (0 g sat),
0 g pro,
0 mg sodium,
3 g carb, 2 g fiber

ACTIVE TIME 10 min.   **TOTAL TIME** 30 min.   **YIELDS** 16 servings (1 Tbsp servings)

INGREDIENTS

- 2 cups raspberries *w/ Tbs. water!*
- 1 Tbsp fresh lemon juice
- 1 Tbsp pure maple syrup
- 2 Tbsp black chia seeds

*Not very good
Runny and tart!
Father's Day 2022*

DIRECTIONS

1. In small saucepan, cook raspberries on medium, stirring occasionally, until fruit breaks down and liquid becomes syrupy, about 8 min. Remove from heat and stir in lemon juice and maple syrup, then stir in chia seeds and let sit 20 min. (mixture should thicken slightly). Store in an airtight container.

CHAPTER ONE: BREAKFAST

Breakfast

Pineapple Cucumber Smoothie

PER SERVING
~180 cal,
4 g fat (1.5 g sat),
8 g pro,
60 mg sodium,
31 g carb, 4 g fiber

Add a tropical twist to your daily smoothie. This one is packed with fiber-rich greens and a punch of protein.

ACTIVE TIME 5 min. **TOTAL TIME** 5 min. **YIELDS** 2 servings

INGREDIENTS

- ½ cup plain Greek yogurt
- ¼ cup unsweetened almond milk or water
- 1 Tbsp fresh lemon juice
- 1 frozen banana, halved
- 1 Persian cucumber, chopped
- 1 cup baby spinach
- 1 cup frozen pineapple chunks

DIRECTIONS

1. Add ingredients to blender in order shown, and puree until smooth.

CHAPTER ONE: BREAKFAST

Breakfast

Peach Mango Smoothie

A quick and easy 4-ingredient pick-me-up.

PER SERVING
~155 cal, 3 g fat (1.5 g sat), 7 g pro, 35 mg sodium, 26 g carb, 3 g fiber

ACTIVE TIME 5 min. **TOTAL TIME** 5 min. **YIELDS** 2 servings

INGREDIENTS

- ½ cup plain Greek yogurt
- ⅓ cup coconut water
- 1 cup frozen sliced peaches
- 1 cup frozen mango chunks

DIRECTIONS

1. Add ingredients to blender in order shown, and puree until smooth.

Breakfast

Winter Citrus Fruit Salad

A medley of succulent citrus lends this salad so much flavor you won't need heavy dressing.

PER SERVING
~85 cal, 1 g fat (0 g sat), 1 g pro, 2 mg sodium, 20 g carb, 3 g fiber

ACTIVE TIME 15 min. **TOTAL TIME** 15 min. **YIELDS** 8 servings

INGREDIENTS

- 1-2 limes
- 1 Tbsp honey
- 2 tsp poppy seeds
- 2 grapefruits (1 red, 1 pink)
- 4 oranges (combination of blood, navel and Cara Cara)
- 1 clementine
- ½ cup pomegranate seeds
- 1 Tbsp fat-free plain yogurt

DIRECTIONS

1. Finely grate 2 tsp lime zest; reserve. Squeeze 3 Tbsp lime juice into small bowl, then whisk in honey and poppy seeds.

2. Cut away peel and white pith of grapefruits, oranges and clementine and slice into rounds. Arrange on platter, drizzle with lime dressing and sprinkle with lime zest and pomegranate seeds. Dollop with yogurt if desired.

Breakfast

Blueberry Banana Nut Smoothie

Smoothies are an easy way to fill up on fruit. The banana, blueberry and almond butter combo in this one has an irresistible creamy texture.

PER SERVING
~190 cal,
11 g fat (1 g sat),
5 g pro,
90 mg sodium,
22 g carb, 5 g fiber

ACTIVE TIME 5 min.   **TOTAL TIME** 5 min.   **YIELDS** 2 servings

INGREDIENTS

- 1 cup unsweetened almond milk
- 2 Tbsp almond butter
- 1 frozen banana
- ½ cup frozen blueberries

DIRECTIONS

1. Add ingredients to blender in order shown, and puree until smooth.

Breakfast

Super-Simple Summer Smoothie

With just three ingredients, this smoothie is a fast and easy way to get your nutrition on the go. Swap in your favorite summer fruit—you can't go wrong!

PER SERVING
~233 cal, 7 g fat (4 g sat), 9 g pro, 85 mg sodium, 37 g carb, 10 g fiber

ACTIVE TIME 5 min. **TOTAL TIME** 5 min. **YIELDS** 1 serving

INGREDIENTS

- ½ cup frozen blueberries
- ¼ cup milk (dairy or nondairy)
- 2 cups fresh summer fruit (blackberries, raspberries, hulled strawberries, chopped peaches and/or nectarines), chilled

DIRECTIONS

1. Add ingredients to blender in order listed and puree until smooth.

Breakfast

Shakshuka

This warming, tomato-centric meal originated in North Africa and is enjoyed throughout most Middle Eastern countries as an easy, healthy breakfast dish. But honestly, it's delicious any time of day (breakfast-for-dinner lovers, we see you!).

PER SERVING
~235 cal, 16.5 g fat (4 g sat), 14 g pro, 390 mg sodium, 8 g carb, 2 g fiber

ACTIVE TIME 15 min. **TOTAL TIME** 35 min. **YIELDS** 4 servings

INGREDIENTS

- 2 Tbsp olive oil
- 1 yellow onion, finely chopped
- 1 clove garlic, finely chopped
- 1 tsp ground cumin
- Kosher salt and pepper
- 1 lb tomatoes, halved if large
- 8 large eggs
- ¼ cup baby spinach, finely chopped
- Toasted baguette, for serving

DIRECTIONS

1. Heat oven to 400°F. Heat oil in large oven-safe skillet on medium. Add onion and sauté until golden brown and tender, 8 min. Stir in garlic, cumin and ½ tsp each salt and pepper and cook 1 min. Stir in tomatoes, then transfer to oven and roast 10 min.

2. Remove pan from oven, stir, then make 8 small wells in vegetable mixture. Carefully crack 1 egg into each. Bake eggs to desired doneness; 7 to 8 min. results in slightly runny yolks. Sprinkle with spinach and, if desired, serve with toast.

CHAPTER ONE: BREAKFAST

Breakfast

Breakfast Tacos

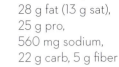

PER SERVING
~435 cal,
28 g fat (13 g sat),
25 g pro,
560 mg sodium,
22 g carb, 5 g fiber

Fresh cilantro and lime juice add a burst of flavor to this crowd-pleasing dish without adding calories.

ACTIVE TIME 15 min.   **TOTAL TIME** 20 min.   **YIELDS** 4 servings

INGREDIENTS

- 8 oz tomatillos (about 10 small), husks discarded
- 1 jalapeño, halved and seeded
- 1 Tbsp olive oil
- Kosher salt
- 8 small corn tortillas
- 6 oz sharp Cheddar cheese, coarsely grated (about 2 cups)
- 8 large eggs
- 2 cups fresh cilantro
- 2 Tbsp lime juice
- Cooked bacon and sliced radishes, for topping

DIRECTIONS

1. Arrange one oven rack 6 in. from broiler and another below that, about 12 in. from broiler; heat broiler. On large rimmed baking sheet, toss tomatillos and jalapeño with oil and pinch salt. Broil on top rack until tender and charred in spots, 8 to 10 min. Transfer to blender.

2. Meanwhile, place tortillas on second large rimmed baking sheet. Top each tortilla with ¼ cup cheese, leaving slight well in center. Top each with one egg (cheese should prevent egg from spilling off tortilla). Broil on middle rack to desired doneness, about 4 to 6 min. for a runny yolk.

3. Add cilantro, lime juice and ¼ tsp salt to vegetables in blender and puree until smooth. Serve salsa on tacos with bacon and radishes if desired.

TIP

To speed things up, make the tomatillo salsa in advance. Just broil a few tomatillos and one jalapeño until they're charred in spots, then blend them together with a few handfuls of fresh cilantro and a good amount of lime juice.

Breakfast

Almond-Berry French Toast Bake

You'll never go back to flipping individual slices after this bountiful bake. Whole grains provide protein and fiber, which slow the absorption of sugar into your bloodstream—ideal for all-day energy.

PER SERVING
~240 cal,
7.5 g fat (2 g sat),
12 g pro,
345 mg sodium,
32 g carb, 6 g fiber

ACTIVE TIME 25 min.   **TOTAL TIME** 1 hr., plus 3 hr. chilling   **YIELDS** 9 servings

INGREDIENTS

- 12 slices stale whole-wheat bread, cut into 1½-in. cubes
- 6-8 oz raspberries
- 6 large eggs
- 2 large egg whites
- 2¼ cups 2% milk
- 3 Tbsp pure maple syrup
- 2 tsp pure vanilla extract
- ¾ tsp ground cinnamon
- ½ tsp kosher salt
- ¼ cup old-fashioned oats
- ¼ cup sliced almonds

DIRECTIONS

1. Lightly coat shallow 1½-qt baking dish with cooking spray. Scatter bread cubes and raspberries in even layer.

2. In large bowl, whisk together eggs, egg whites, milk, maple syrup, vanilla, cinnamon and salt. Pour mixture over top of bread cubes, cover, and refrigerate 3 hr.

3. Heat oven to 350°F. Sprinkle oats and almonds over top and bake until puffed and golden brown, 40 to 50 min.

Top w/ whip cream instead of syrup

Breakfast

Very Berry Quinoa Muffins

Warming spices, whole grains and yogurt create a comforting and healthy way to start the day. Bookmark this recipe for the next time you have extra raspberries you need to use up!

PER SERVING
~170 cal,
7 g fat (1 g sat),
6 g pro,
205 mg sodium,
23 g carb, 3 g fiber

ACTIVE TIME 10 min.   **TOTAL TIME** 30 min.   **YIELDS** 12 servings

INGREDIENTS

- ¾ cup all-purpose flour, plus more for dusting
- 1 cup almond flour
- ¼ cup uncooked white quinoa
- 1 tsp baking powder
- 1 tsp ground cinnamon
- ½ tsp ground ginger
- ½ tsp baking soda
- ½ tsp kosher salt
- 2 large eggs, beaten
- 1 cup plain full-fat yogurt
- ¼ cup whole milk
- ⅓ cup honey
- 2 6-oz containers small raspberries

DIRECTIONS

1. Heat oven to 325°F. Lightly coat 12-cup muffin pan with cooking spray and dust with flour.

2. In large bowl, whisk together flours, quinoa, baking powder, cinnamon, ginger, baking soda and salt.

3. In medium bowl, whisk together eggs, yogurt, milk and honey. Fold egg mixture into flour mixture until just combined, then stir in raspberries.

4. Divide batter among muffin-pan cups and bake until toothpick inserted into centers of muffins comes out clean, 15 to 20 min. Cool in pan 5 min., then transfer to wire rack to cool completely.

Breakfast

Easiest Ever Bagels

Fresh bagels, no boiling necessary! Greek yogurt provides a hunger-fighting boost of protein and all the flavor of your favorite deli version.

PER SERVING
~185 cal,
4 g fat (2 g sat),
10 g pro,
415 mg sodium,
27 g carb, 1 g fiber

ACTIVE TIME 20 min. **TOTAL TIME** 50 min. **YIELDS** 8 servings

INGREDIENTS

- 2 cups self-rising flour, plus more for dusting
- 2 cups plain Greek yogurt
- 1 large egg, beaten
- Sesame seeds, for topping
- Poppy seeds, for topping
- Onion flakes, for topping
- Everything seasoning, for topping

Not very good! Blah 2022

DIRECTIONS

1. Heat oven to 350°F. Line baking sheet with parchment paper.

2. In bowl, combine flour and yogurt until dough starts to form. Turn out dough onto lightly floured surface and knead 2 min.

3. Divide into 8 pieces. Roll each piece of dough into 1-in.-thick log (about 9 in. long) and pinch ends together to form circle. Place on prepared baking sheet.

4. Brush tops of bagels with egg, then sprinkle with desired toppings. Bake until golden brown, 28 to 35 min.

Breakfast

Mason Jar Scramble

Skip the sugary cereal on busy mornings and whip up this quick-cooking, low-fat dish instead. Simply toss all the ingredients in a jar, microwave and enjoy!

PER SERVING
~155 cal, 10 g fat (3.5 g sat), 13 g pro, 275 mg sodium, 2 g carb, 0 g fiber

ACTIVE TIME 5 min. **TOTAL TIME** 10 min. **YIELDS** 1 serving

INGREDIENTS

- 2 large eggs
- 1 Tbsp milk
- Kosher salt and pepper
- ¼ cup baby spinach
- 3 grape tomatoes, quartered
- 2 small basil leaves, torn

DIRECTIONS

1. In a 10- to 12-oz jar, place eggs, milk and pinch each salt and pepper. Screw lid on tightly and shake until well mixed, about 20 seconds. Add baby spinach and shake again.

2. Remove lid and microwave on High for 60 seconds, then in 15-second intervals until just set.

3. Top with grape tomatoes and basil leaves.

TIP
Another tasty topping mixture to try is ⅛ avocado (diced) and ½ scallion (thinly sliced).

Breakfast

Pear & Cottage Cheese Toast

This sweet and savory breakfast toast is high in fiber and protein to keep you full until lunch. Feel free to swap in your favorite gluten-free bread.

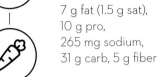

PER SERVING
~220 cal,
7 g fat (1.5 g sat),
10 g pro,
265 mg sodium,
31 g carb, 5 g fiber

ACTIVE TIME 5 min.   **TOTAL TIME** 5 min.   **YIELDS** 1 serving

INGREDIENTS

- 2 slices whole-grain bread
- ⅓ cup small-curd cottage cheese
- ½ ripe pear, sliced
- 1 orange
- 2 Tbsp roasted hazelnuts or sliced almonds
- Honey, optional

DIRECTIONS

1. Toast bread. Spread half cottage cheese on each slice of toast and top with pear slices.

2. Finely grate ½ tsp zest from orange and set aside. Squeeze a touch of orange juice on top of toast slices, then sprinkle with roasted hazelnuts or sliced almonds.

3. Sprinkle with reserved zest and drizzle with honey, if desired.

TIP

Cottage cheese provides a boost of protein (at least 7 grams!) as well as tryptophan, an essential amino acid linked with improved mood and cognition.

Breakfast

Spiced Plum & Quinoa Muffins

PER SERVING
~160 cal,
7 g fat (4 g sat),
4 g pro,
200 mg sodium,
23 g carb, 1 g fiber

Start your morning with these fluffy whole-grain muffins made with cinnamon, ginger and plums. Quinoa sneaks in a dose of protein but blends seamlessly with other ingredients.

ACTIVE TIME 20 min. **TOTAL TIME** 50 min. **YIELDS** 18 servings

INGREDIENTS

- 1 cup all-purpose flour
- 1 cup whole-wheat flour
- 1/3 cup uncooked white quinoa
- 1 tsp baking powder
- 1 tsp ground cinnamon
- 1/2 tsp ground ginger
- 1/2 tsp baking soda
- 1/2 tsp salt
- 2 large eggs, beaten
- 1 cup plain full-fat yogurt
- 1/2 cup (1 stick) butter, melted
- 1/2 cup honey, plus more for drizzling (optional)
- 2 plums, 1 chopped and 1 thinly sliced

DIRECTIONS

1. Preheat oven to 400°F. Line 18 muffin-pan cups with paper liners.

2. In large bowl, whisk flours, quinoa, baking powder, cinnamon, ginger, baking soda and salt.

3. In medium bowl, whisk eggs, yogurt, butter and honey. Fold egg mixture into flour mixture until just combined; stir in chopped plum.

4. Divide batter among muffin cups (about ¼ cup each) and top each with a couple of plum slices.

5. Bake 15 to 20 min. or until toothpick inserted into centers of muffins comes out clean. Cool in pans 5 min., then transfer to wire rack to cool completely.

6. Drizzle with honey, if desired, before serving.

Breakfast

Spinach & Goat Cheese Egg Muffins

These easy egg muffins contain the ultimate trio: protein-packed eggs, nutrient-rich veggies and flavorful goat cheese. It all adds up to a tasty and healthy morning meal.

PER SERVING
~65 cal,
4.5 g fat (1.5 g sat),
4 g pro,
120 mg sodium,
2 g carb, 1 g fiber

ACTIVE TIME 25 min.   **TOTAL TIME** 45 min.   **YIELDS** 12 servings

INGREDIENTS

 ½

- 1 Tbsp olive oil
- 1 large red pepper, cut into ¼-in. pieces
- Kosher salt and pepper
- 2 scallions, chopped
- 6 large eggs
- ½ cup milk
- 1 5-oz pkg. baby spinach, chopped
- ¼ cup fresh goat cheese, crumbled
- *Bacon*

DIRECTIONS

1. Heat oven to 350°F. Spray 12-cup muffin pan with nonstick cooking spray.

2. Heat oil in large skillet on medium. Add red pepper and ⅛ tsp each salt and pepper and cook, covered, stirring occasionally, until tender, 6 to 8 min. Remove from heat and stir in scallions.

3. In large bowl, beat together eggs, milk, ¼ tsp salt and ⅛ tsp pepper. Stir in spinach and red pepper mixture.

4. Divide batter among muffin pan cups (about ¼ cup each), top with goat cheese and bake until just set in center, 20 to 25 min. (Even when set, tops of frittatas may look wet from spinach.)

5. Cool on wire rack 5 min., then remove from pan. Serve warm. Can be refrigerated up to 4 days; microwave on high 30 seconds to reheat.

TIP
Meal-prep these on Sunday for a quick, portable breakfast all week.

Breakfast

Fruit & Nut Bars

PER SERVING
~214 cal,
10.5 g fat (1.5 g sat),
5 g pro,
38 mg sodium,
28 g carb, 4 g fiber

Lightly sweet, these hearty no-bake bars cut out the added sugar but are full of flavor. The secret's in the mix: dried cranberries, golden raisins, apricots and dates.

ACTIVE TIME 15 min. **TOTAL TIME** 45 min. **YIELDS** 12 servings

---

INGREDIENTS

- 1 cup pitted dates (about 12)
- ¼ cup peanut or almond butter
- ¼ cup honey
- 1 tsp pure vanilla extract
- 1 cup roasted unsalted almonds, roughly chopped
- ½ cup rolled oats
- ¾ cup dried fruit (cranberries, golden raisins, sliced apricots)
- ¼ cup pumpkin seeds

DIRECTIONS

1. Line 8-in. square pan with nonstick foil, leaving overhang on all sides.

2. In food processor, chop dates (they will form a ball); transfer to bowl.

3. In small saucepan over medium heat, melt peanut butter, honey and vanilla, stirring occasionally, until combined, about 1 min. Add to bowl with dates and mix to combine.

4. Fold in almonds, oats, dried fruit and pumpkin seeds. Press mixture into prepared pan and freeze until sliceable, about 30 min. Cut into 12 bars. Store in refrigerator.

Chapter Two
Lunch

Sheet Pan Chicken Fajitas
p. 133

Lunch

Butternut Squash & Spinach Toasts

PER SERVING
~343 cal,
15.5 g fat (4.5 g sat),
17 g pro,
480 mg sodium,
37 g carb, 7 g fiber

A fall favorite, this satisfying toast features potassium-rich butternut squash as the star ingredient. The egg on top makes it a nutritionally balanced meal.

ACTIVE TIME 20 min.   **TOTAL TIME** 20 min.   **YIELDS** 4 servings

INGREDIENTS

- 1 large butternut squash
- 1 Tbsp oil
- 2 cloves garlic, chopped
- 1 bunch spinach, roughly chopped
- Kosher salt and pepper
- 4 pieces toast
- 1/3 cup grated Gruyère
- 4 large eggs

DIRECTIONS

1. Cut neck off large butternut squash (reserve other half for another use). Peel and cut into ½-in. pieces.

2. In large nonstick skillet over medium heat, heat oil. Add squash, cover and cook, stirring occasionally, for 8 min. Add garlic and cook uncovered, stirring occasionally, until squash is golden brown and just tender.

3. Add spinach, season with ¼ tsp each salt and pepper and toss until spinach is beginning to wilt, 1 to 2 min.

4. In a second nonstick skillet, fry eggs to desired doneness. Top toast with Gruyère, squash, and fried egg.

Lunch

Charred Scallion Tart

Cheese, onions and herbs come together to create a light and clean main or side dish, perfect for spring or any time of year. Pair with a salad as a delicious lunch option.

PER SERVING
~310 cal, 20 g fat (10 g sat), 11 g pro, 440 mg sodium, 28 g carb, 3 g fiber

ACTIVE TIME 30 min. **TOTAL TIME** 30 min. **YIELDS** 6-8 servings

INGREDIENTS

- 1 sheet frozen puff pastry, thawed
- Milk or beaten egg, for brushing
- 3 bunches scallions, trimmed; reserve 1 scallion and chop it finely
- Oil, for brushing
- 8 oz fresh goat cheese, at room temperature
- ½ cup whole-milk ricotta cheese
- ¼ cup fresh flat-leaf parsley, chopped, plus more for topping
- ¼ cup fresh mint, chopped, plus more for topping
- 2 Tbsp lemon juice
- 2 tsp grated lemon zest, plus more zest for topping
- Kosher salt and pepper
- Chopped toasted almonds, for topping

DIRECTIONS

1. Place oven rack in lower third of oven; heat oven to 400°F. Unfold pastry onto piece of parchment paper and roll ½ in. bigger on all sides. Slide parchment and pastry onto baking sheet. Using sharp knife, score a ½-in. border all around edges, then score border at 1-in. increments at a diagonal. Brush border with milk or beaten egg. Using fork, prick middle of pastry all over. Bake until deep golden brown, 18 to 25 min. (Don't worry if middle puffs; you can push it down once it cools.)

2. Meanwhile, heat large cast iron skillet on medium-high. Brush whole scallions with oil and season with ½ tsp each salt and pepper. Cook in batches, turning occasionally, until charred and whites are slightly tender; transfer to plate and repeat with remaining scallions.

3. In food processor, pulse goat cheese and ricotta until smooth. Add parsley, mint, lemon juice and zest, chopped scallion and ¼ tsp each salt and pepper and pulse briefly to combine. Gently spread in center of cooled pastry and arrange charred scallions on top. Sprinkle with additional herbs and lemon zest and almonds, if desired.

Lunch

Spring Panzanella

There may be sourdough in this recipe, but with scallions, peas, fresh herbs and greens tossed in a bright vinaigrette, it totally counts as a salad.

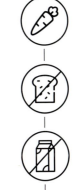

PER SERVING
~235 cal, 10.5 g fat (1.5 g sat), 7 g pro, 505 mg sodium, 29 g carb, 3 g fiber

ACTIVE TIME 20 min. **TOTAL TIME** 20 min. **YIELDS** 6 servings

INGREDIENTS

- ½ small loaf (about 12 oz) sourdough bread, preferably stale, crusts trimmed, torn into large pieces
- 4 Tbsp olive oil, divided
- 2 Tbsp white wine vinegar
- 2 tsp Dijon mustard
- Kosher salt and pepper
- 2 scallions, white and light green parts finely chopped, dark green parts thinly sliced
- 2 Persian cucumbers, smashed, halved lengthwise and then sliced
- ½ cup fresh or frozen peas (thawed if frozen)
- 2 cups mixed fresh herbs (such as parsley, basil, mint, dill)
- 5 oz mixed greens

DIRECTIONS

1. Heat oven to 400°F. On rimmed baking sheet, toss bread with 1 Tbsp oil and roast until golden brown, about 10 min.

2. Meanwhile, in large bowl, whisk together vinegar, mustard, remaining 3 Tbsp oil and ½ tsp each salt and pepper; stir in chopped scallions.

3. Add cucumber and toss to coat, then toss with toasted bread. Add peas, herbs and greens and toss gently to combine.

Lunch

Roasted Butternut Squash Salad
with Tahini Vinaigrette

Drizzled with a tahini dressing, this simple salad has all of the best flavors of fall, but its hearty bite, protein and fiber satisfy any time of year.

PER SERVING
~270 cal,
18 g fat (2.5 g sat),
7 g pro,
280 mg sodium,
25 g carb, 7 g fiber

ACTIVE TIME 20 min.   **TOTAL TIME** 45 min.   **YIELDS** 4 servings

INGREDIENTS

- 1 small butternut squash (about 1¼ lbs), cut into ½-in.-thick wedges or half moons
- 2 medium red onions, cut into 1-in. wedges
- 2 Tbsp olive oil
- Kosher salt and pepper
- ¼ cup tahini
- 2 Tbsp lemon juice
- 2 Tbsp water
- 4 cups baby kale
- 2 tsp grated lemon zest
- ¼ cup cilantro, chopped
- ¼ cup sliced almonds, toasted

w/ grilled pork chop

DIRECTIONS

1. Heat oven to 450°F. On large rimmed baking sheet, toss squash and onions with oil and ¼ tsp each salt and pepper. Roast until golden brown and tender, 25 to 35 min.

2. Meanwhile, in small bowl, whisk together tahini, lemon juice, water and ¼ tsp salt, adding additional water if dressing is too thick.

3. Toss squash with kale and arrange on platter. Drizzle with dressing and sprinkle with lemon zest, cilantro and almonds.

Lunch

Quinoa-Stuffed Acorn Squash
with Cranberries & Feta

Packed with antioxidant-rich berries, Swiss chard and 100% whole grains, this vegetarian main is hefty enough to keep you satisfied—and it's good for your heart, too.

PER SERVING
~260 cal,
7 g fat (1 g sat),
5 g pro,
255 mg sodium,
49 g carb, 10 g fiber

ACTIVE TIME 10 min.   **TOTAL TIME** 45 min.   **YIELDS** 8 servings

INGREDIENTS

- 4 small acorn squash (about 4½ lbs)
- 3 Tbsp olive oil, divided
- Kosher salt and pepper
- 1 medium onion, finely chopped
- 2 cloves garlic, finely chopped
- 1 cup mixed-color quinoa
- 2 tsp fresh thyme leaves
- ⅓ cup dried cranberries
- 1 small bunch Swiss chard, stems discarded, leaves roughly chopped (about 6 cups)
- Crumbled feta cheese, for serving

DIRECTIONS

1. Place rimmed baking sheet in oven and heat oven to 425°F. Prep squash: cut ½ in. from each pointy end, then halve each through its center (this will help them stand straight); scrape out and discard seeds. Rub squash with 1 Tbsp oil and season with ¼ tsp each salt and pepper. Arrange on baking sheet and roast, hollow side down, until tender, 25 to 30 min.

2. Meanwhile, in 3- to 4-qt saucepan, heat remaining 2 Tbsp oil on medium. Add onion and ½ tsp each salt and pepper. Cook, covered, stirring often, for 7 min. Stir in garlic; cook 2 min.

3. Add quinoa and toss to coat, then add thyme and 2 cups water. Simmer, covered, for 10 min. Stir in cranberries. Simmer, covered, for 5 min.

4. Remove from heat; place Swiss chard on top of quinoa and cover pot with clean dish towel, then lid. Let stand 10 min.

5. Transfer squash to platter, hollow sides up. Fold chard into quinoa, then spoon into squash halves. Top with feta, if desired.

Lunch

Hot Pepper & Onion Pizza

PER SERVING
~330 cal,
6.5 g fat (1.5 g sat),
12 g pro,
690 mg sodium,
57 g carb, 3 g fiber

Pizza can be low-cal-friendly if you pile on nutritious veggies. Peppers not only add color to this dish, but as one of the richest sources of vitamin C they also add a nutrient boost.

ACTIVE TIME 15 min.   **TOTAL TIME** 30 min.   **YIELDS** 4 servings

INGREDIENTS

- 1 lb pizza dough
- Cornmeal, for dusting
- 1 small onion, thinly sliced
- 1 small red pepper, sliced
- 1 small yellow pepper, sliced
- 1 poblano pepper, halved and thinly sliced
- 1 small jalapeño, halved and thinly sliced
- 1 Tbsp olive oil
- Kosher salt and pepper
- 1½ oz extra-sharp Cheddar, coarsely grated

DIRECTIONS

1. Heat oven to 500°F (if you can't heat your oven this high without broiling, heat it to 475°F).

2. On lightly floured surface, shape pizza dough into 14-in. oval. Place on cornmeal-dusted baking sheet.

3. In bowl, toss onion, all peppers, olive oil, plus ¼ tsp each salt and pepper. Sprinkle Cheddar over dough, then scatter pepper mixture on top.

4. Bake until crust is golden brown, 10 to 12 min.

TIP

Switch it up! Vary types (and colors) of peppers to give your 'za more layers of flavor. Spicier peppers, like jalapeños, offer a contrast to the creaminess of the cheese.

Lunch

Vegetable Torte

Tortes are the ideal foundation for a variety of vegetables. This one ups the flavor with sharp provolone and grated Parmesan.

PER SERVING
~140 cal,
7 g fat (3.5 g sat),
7 g pro,
305 mg sodium,
14 g carb, 2 g fiber

ACTIVE TIME 15 min. **TOTAL TIME** 45 min. **YIELDS** 8 servings

---

INGREDIENTS

- 1 Tbsp olive oil, divided, plus more for pan
- ½ small butternut squash (about 1 lb), peeled and thinly sliced
- 1 red onion, thinly sliced
- 1 small bunch kale, thick stems discarded and leaves cut into 1-in. pieces
- Kosher salt and pepper
- 1 medium yellow potato (about 6 oz), thinly sliced
- 4 oz thinly sliced sharp provolone cheese
- 1 plum tomato, thinly sliced
- 1 oz Parmesan cheese, grated (about ¼ cup)

DIRECTIONS

1. Heat oven to 425°F. Oil 9-in. springform pan. Arrange half of squash in bottom of pan, in concentric circles. Top with half of onion, then half of kale. Drizzle with ½ Tbsp oil and season with ¼ tsp salt. Top with potato and half of provolone cheese.

2. Top with remaining kale, drizzle with remaining ½ Tbsp oil and season with ¼ tsp each salt and pepper. Top with remaining onion, tomato and remaining provolone. Arrange remaining squash on top and sprinkle with Parmesan.

3. Cover with foil, place on baking sheet and bake 20 min. Uncover and bake until tender and top is browned, 8 to 10 min.

Lunch

White Bean & Tuna Salad

with Basil Vinaigrette

This quick lunch takes the humble can of tuna to new heights. The herby dressing delivers major flavor while the soft-boiled eggs up the protein to a whopping 31 grams.

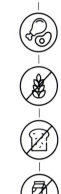

PER SERVING
~340 cal,
16.5 g fat (3 g sat),
31 g pro,
770 mg sodium,
24 g carb, 8 g fiber

ACTIVE TIME 25 min. **TOTAL TIME** 25 min. **YIELDS** 4 servings

---

INGREDIENTS

- Kosher salt and pepper
- 12 oz green beans, trimmed and halved
- 1 small shallot, chopped
- 1 cup lightly packed basil leaves
- 3 Tbsp olive oil
- 1 Tbsp red wine vinegar
- 4 cups torn lettuce
- 1 15-oz can small white beans, rinsed
- 2 5-oz cans solid white tuna in water, drained
- 4 soft-boiled eggs, halved

DIRECTIONS

1. Bring large pot of water to a boil. Add 1 Tbsp salt, then green beans and cook until just tender, 3 to 4 min. Drain and rinse under cold water to cool.

2. Meanwhile, in blender, puree shallot, basil, oil, vinegar and ½ tsp each salt and pepper until smooth.

3. Transfer half of dressing to large bowl and toss with green beans. Fold in lettuce, white beans and tuna and serve with remaining dressing and eggs.

Lunch

Seared Coconut Lime Chicken
with Snap Pea Slaw

This one-skillet meal incorporates a splash of coconut cream and fresh lime juice to create a creamy and tangy low-carb dish.

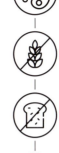

PER SERVING
~290 cal,
15 g fat (3.5 g sat),
29 g pro,
540 mg sodium,
10 g carb, 3 g fiber

ACTIVE TIME 45 min. **TOTAL TIME** 45 min. **YIELDS** 4 servings

INGREDIENTS

- 2 Tbsp toasted sesame oil
- 1 Tbsp grated fresh ginger
- 3 Tbsp fresh lime juice, divided (from about 2 limes)
- Kosher salt and pepper
- 10 oz snap peas, strings removed and thinly sliced
- 4 oz snow peas, thinly sliced
- 2 scallions, thinly sliced
- 2 8-oz boneless, skinless chicken breasts
- 1 Tbsp olive oil
- 2 Tbsp coconut cream
- ½ cup ~~cilantro~~ *parsley*

DIRECTIONS

1. In large bowl, whisk together sesame oil, ginger, 1½ Tbsp lime juice and ½ tsp salt. Add snap peas, snow peas and scallions, and toss to combine.

2. Cut each breast horizontally in half to make 4 thin cutlets, then pound to ¼ in. thick. Heat oil in large skillet on medium-high. Season chicken with ½ tsp each salt and pepper and cook in batches until golden brown and cooked through, about 2 min. per side. Transfer chicken to plates as it is cooked. Remove pan from heat and stir in coconut cream and remaining 1½ Tbsp lime juice, scraping up any browned bits. Spoon over chicken on plates.

3. Fold cilantro into pea mixture and serve on top of chicken.

Really good! Added sesame seeds and pure maple syrup. June 2022

CHAPTER TWO: LUNCH

Lunch

Grilled Eggplant
with Chickpea Croutons

Skip the bread! Chickpea croutons make this summer side dish gluten-free but still full of flavor.

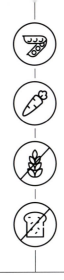

PER SERVING
~255 cal,
13.5 g fat (2 g sat),
8 g pro,
210 mg sodium,
27 g carb, 8 g fiber

ACTIVE TIME 35 min.   **TOTAL TIME** 1 hr. 10 min.   **YIELDS** 4 servings

INGREDIENTS

- 3 Tbsp plus 1 tsp olive oil, divided
- 1 small onion, finely chopped
- 2 cloves garlic, pressed, divided
- Kosher salt
- 1 cup chickpea flour
- 1 Tbsp lemon zest
- 2 medium eggplants (about 12 oz each), cut lengthwise into ½-in. slices
- ¼ cup plain full-fat yogurt
- 2 tsp lemon juice
- 1 cup mint leaves, torn
- 2 Tbsp chopped chives

DIRECTIONS

1. Line 4½- by 8½-in. loaf pan with parchment, leaving overhang on two long sides. Heat 1 Tbsp oil in large saucepan on medium. Add onion, half garlic and ¼ tsp salt and cook, stirring occasionally, until tender, 5 min. Add 2 cups water and bring to a boil. While whisking, slowly stream in chickpea flour and whisk vigorously, off heat, until mostly lump-free.

2. Transfer mixture to food processor with lemon zest and puree, gradually adding 1 Tbsp oil until completely smooth. Immediately transfer to prepared pan and smooth top. Cover with another piece of parchment and another loaf pan and press with heavy object. Refrigerate until firm, 30 min. to 1 hr.

3. Meanwhile, heat grill to medium-high. Cut chickpea mixture into ½-in. cubes. Heat 1 tsp oil in small skillet and cook in 2 to 3 batches, turning occasionally, until browned, 3 to 5 min. Transfer to paper towel to drain.

4. Brush eggplant slices with remaining Tbsp oil, season with pinch of salt and grill until tender and lightly charred, about 3 min. per side. Place on platter.

5. In small bowl, whisk together yogurt, lemon juice, remaining garlic and pinch salt. Drizzle yogurt sauce over eggplant and sprinkle with chickpea croutons, mint and chives.

Lunch

Grilled Green Beans, Fennel & Farro

No more boring boiled beans with this high-fiber grilled vegetarian dish. A couple tablespoons of white wine vinegar makes all the difference.

PER SERVING
~230 cal,
11 g fat (1.5 g sat),
7 g pro,
450 mg sodium,
30 g carb, 7 g fiber

ACTIVE TIME 20 min.   **TOTAL TIME** 25 min.   **YIELDS** 4 servings

INGREDIENTS

- ½ cup quick-cooking farro [Barley]
- ½ lb green beans, trimmed
- ½ lb wax beans, trimmed
- 2 Tbsp olive oil, divided
- Kosher salt
- 1 Tbsp fennel seeds
- Pinch red pepper flakes
- 2 Tbsp white wine vinegar
- 1 tsp honey
- ¼ cup toasted pistachios, chopped
- 1 small bulb fennel, very thinly shaved
- Fennel fronds, for topping

Add ground Tky ranch seasoning

DIRECTIONS

1. Heat grill to medium-high. Cook farro per package directions. Drain, transfer to large bowl and let cool to room temperature.

2. In second large bowl, toss green and wax beans with ½ Tbsp oil and ¼ tsp salt. Grill, turning occasionally, until just tender, 4 to 6 min. Transfer to bowl with farro.

3. In small skillet on medium, toast fennel seeds and pepper flakes until fragrant. Let cool, then pulse in spice grinder (or crush with side of heavy skillet) until mostly cracked.

4. Meanwhile, in small bowl, whisk together vinegar, honey, remaining 1½ Tbsp oil and ¼ tsp salt. Stir in fennel seed mixture and pistachios. Toss farro and beans with dressing and fold in fennel. Serve topped with fennel fronds if desired.

Lunch

Peach & Prosciutto Flatbreads

PER SERVING
~235 cal,
7.5 g fat (2.5 g sat),
11 g pro,
905 mg sodium,
30 g carb, 2 g fiber

Who knew everything you needed to make your pizzas taste wood-fired was already in your backyard? Fire up your grill to give these flatbreads a beautiful char.

ACTIVE TIME 40 min. **TOTAL TIME** 40 min. **YIELDS** 8 servings

INGREDIENTS

- 1 lb pizza dough
- 5 tsp olive oil, divided
- 3 peaches or nectarines, each pitted and cut into 8 wedges
- Kosher salt and pepper
- 2 Tbsp fresh lemon juice
- 2 tsp chopped tarragon
- 3 oz Gruyère cheese, grated
- 2 cups baby arugula
- 4 oz prosciutto, thinly sliced

DIRECTIONS

1. Heat grill to medium-high and arrange so half will give direct heat and other half will give indirect heat. Working on floured surface, divide pizza dough in half and shape each piece into 5- by 14-in. oval or rectangle and place on flour-dusted baking sheet. Brush each top with 2 tsp oil.

2. Toss peaches with 1 tsp oil and ¼ tsp each salt and pepper. Grill peaches over direct heat until lightly charred, 2 to 3 min. per side. Transfer peaches to large bowl.

3. Transfer pizza dough to grill over direct heat, oiled side down, and grill, covered, until top begins to bubble and bottom is crisp, 2 min. (use tongs to peek underneath). Working quickly, brush tops of dough with remaining 2 tsp oil. Flip dough to indirect-heat side of grill, then grill, covered, until dough is cooked through and charred in spots on bottom, 3 to 5 min. more; transfer to cutting board.

4. Toss peaches with lemon juice, tarragon and pinch each salt and pepper. Sprinkle Gruyère over dough and grill, covered, until melted, 2 to 3 min.

5. Add arugula to peaches and toss to coat. Top cheesy pizza dough with prosciutto and peach-arugula salad.

Lunch

Tuscan-Style Tomato & Bread Salad

PER SERVING
~400 cal,
22 g fat (4.5 g sat),
15 g pro,
711 mg sodium,
37 g carb, 4 g fiber

Yes, we said "bread salad." Mixed with antioxidant-rich tomatoes and topped with an egg for a protein boost, the baguette balances out the meal and makes it extra hearty.

ACTIVE TIME 15 min.   **TOTAL TIME** 20 min.   **YIELDS** 4 servings

INGREDIENTS

- 1 lb cherry tomatoes, halved
- ½ small red onion, thinly sliced
- 1½ Tbsp red wine vinegar
- 4 Tbsp olive oil, divided
- Kosher salt and pepper
- 1 baguette, roughly torn
- 1 clove garlic, finely grated
- 3 cups baby spinach
- 3 cups baby kale
- 4 sunny-side-up eggs

DIRECTIONS

1. In large bowl, toss tomatoes and onion with red wine vinegar, 3 Tbsp oil and ½ tsp each salt and pepper; let sit 10 min.

2. Heat oven to 400°F. On rimmed baking sheet, toss baguette pieces with garlic and remaining Tbsp oil and roast until golden brown, 8 to 10 min.

3. Toss toasted bread with tomato mixture, then fold in spinach and kale. Top each serving with 1 egg, if desired.

Lunch

Chicken Soup
with Spinach & Lemon

Two large eggs whisked into this easy soup provide body and richness without any cream. It's the lemony, light lunch you'll make on repeat.

PER SERVING
~270 cal,
6.5 g fat (1.5 g sat),
38 g pro,
410 mg sodium,
14 g carb, 4 g fiber

ACTIVE TIME 25 min. **TOTAL TIME** 1 hr. **YIELDS** 4 servings

INGREDIENTS

- 2 large yellow onions, halved
- 1 head garlic, halved
- 1 rind Parmesan cheese
- Kosher salt and pepper
- 3 small boneless, skinless chicken breasts (1¼ lbs)
- 2 large eggs
- 6 Tbsp fresh lemon juice, plus zest for serving
- 6 cups baby spinach

DIRECTIONS

1. In large pot, simmer onions, garlic, Parmesan rind and 12 cups water for 25 min. Over large bowl, strain out solids and return liquid to pot. Season with ½ tsp each salt and pepper and return to simmer. Add chicken and poach until cooked through, 11 to 13 min. Using tongs, transfer chicken to bowl (do not discard broth). Let cool slightly and shred into pieces.

2. Meanwhile, in medium bowl, whisk together eggs and lemon juice until foamy. Slowly, 1 Tbsp at a time, whisk in 1 cup of broth from pot. While whisking broth in pot constantly, slowly add egg broth mixture to pot. Reduce heat to medium-low and cook until soup is slightly thickened and velvety, about 5 min. Remove from heat, stir in chicken and spinach and let sit 5 min. before serving.

3. Spoon into bowls and serve sprinkled with lemon zest and cracked pepper, if desired.

Lunch

Charred Shrimp, Leek & Asparagus Skewers

You can stack your skewers high without piling on calories when you use a combo of spring vegetables and succulent shrimp. The harissa-based sauce adds a creamy kick.

PER SERVING
~370 cal,
28.5 g fat (4.5 g sat),
18 g pro,
1,110 mg sodium,
12 g carb, 2 g fiber

ACTIVE TIME 30 min. **TOTAL TIME** 30 min. **YIELDS** 4 servings

INGREDIENTS

- 1 lb (21–25) peeled and deveined shrimp
- 1 lb asparagus, trimmed and cut into 2-in. pieces
- 2 medium leeks, white and light green parts only, cut into ¾-in.-thick rounds
- 2 Tbsp olive oil
- Kosher salt and pepper
- 2 lemons, halved
- ½ cup mayonnaise
- 1½ Tbsp harissa paste

DIRECTIONS

1. Heat grill to medium-high. Thread shrimp, asparagus and leek rounds onto skewers. Brush lightly with oil and season with ½ tsp each salt and pepper.

2. Grill skewers until vegetables are tender and shrimp are opaque throughout, 3 to 4 min. per side.

3. Place lemons on grill alongside skewers, cut sides down, and grill until charred, about 4 min.

4. Into small bowl, squeeze 2 tsp juice from 1 charred lemon half. Stir in mayonnaise and harissa to combine. Serve skewers with harissa mayo and remaining charred lemon halves.

Lunch

Rhubarb & Citrus Salad

with Black Pepper Vinaigrette

An easy way to eat antioxidant-rich rhubarb, this salad has a sweet and savory crunch with a pleasingly peppery finish.

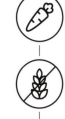

PER SERVING
~280 cal,
19.5 g fat (3.5 g sat),
5 g pro,
380 mg sodium,
25 g carb, 4 g fiber

ACTIVE TIME 25 min.   **TOTAL TIME** 1 hr.   **YIELDS** 4 servings

INGREDIENTS

- 2 Tbsp honey
- 2 Tbsp white wine vinegar
- 3 stalks rhubarb, trimmed and cut into 1-in. pieces
- ¼ cup olive oil
- Kosher salt and pepper
- 3 oz baby spinach (about 4 cups)
- 2 bunches watercress, thick stems removed
- 2 Cara Cara oranges, peel and pith trimmed, sliced
- ¼ cup toasted pistachios, chopped
- 1 oz ricotta salata, shaved

DIRECTIONS

1. In small bowl, whisk together honey and vinegar. Add rhubarb and toss to coat. Let stand at least 5 min. and up to 10 min., then add olive oil, ½ tsp salt and 2 tsp coarsely ground pepper.

2. In large bowl, toss spinach and watercress; fold in orange slices and divide among plates. Spoon rhubarb and dressing over each salad and top with pistachios and ricotta salata.

Lunch

Cauliflower Fried Rice

Say goodbye to takeout—this easy, vegetarian fried rice recipe is bursting with flavor thanks to ginger, honey and edamame.

PER SERVING
~251 cal,
13.5 g fat (2 g sat),
15 g pro,
449 mg sodium,
20 g carb, 6 g fiber

ACTIVE TIME 20 min.   **TOTAL TIME** 20 min.   **YIELDS** 4 servings

INGREDIENTS

- ½ large head cauliflower
- 2 Tbsp vegetable oil, divided
- 1 orange pepper, cut into thin ½-in. pieces
- 1 scallion, thinly sliced, divided
- 1 2-in. piece ginger, cut into thin matchsticks
- 2 Tbsp low-sodium soy sauce
- 2 tsp chili garlic paste
- 2 tsp honey
- 4 large eggs
- 1 cup frozen peas, thawed
- 1 cup frozen edamame, thawed
- Lime wedges, for serving

DIRECTIONS

1. Cut cauliflower into florets, discarding tough inner core and leaves. Working in batches, transfer cauliflower to bowl of food processor. Pulse until cauliflower resembles rice, about 15 seconds (be careful not to over-process or cauliflower will get mushy). Set aside, then repeat with remaining cauliflower (you should have about 4 cups of cauliflower).

2. Heat 1 Tbsp oil in large cast-iron skillet over medium-high heat. Add pepper, white parts of scallion and ginger; cook, stirring, 2 min. Add cauliflower, toss to combine and cook, covered, stirring once, for 5 min.

3. Meanwhile, in small bowl, whisk together soy sauce, chili garlic paste and honey. In separate small bowl, lightly beat eggs. Push cauliflower mixture to one side of skillet, add remaining 1 Tbsp oil, then eggs, and scramble until cooked, 2 min.

4. Remove skillet from heat, and fold in eggs, sauce, peas and edamame. Serve with thinly sliced scallion greens and lime wedges.

Lunch

Shrimp Ceviche

Shrimp ceviche generally calls for raw shrimp marinated in lime juice, then tossed with fresh veggies and avocado. We kept the citrus but cooked the shrimp to bring out even more flavor.

PER SERVING
~210 cal,
8.5 g fat (1 g sat),
21 g pro,
525 mg sodium,
14 g carb, 4 g fiber

ACTIVE TIME 20 min. **TOTAL TIME** 20 min. **YIELDS** 4 servings

INGREDIENTS

- 6 Tbsp fresh lime juice (from 2 or 3 limes)
- ½ cup fresh Cara Cara orange juice (from 1 orange) plus 1 orange, cut into segments
- 1 tsp honey
- Kosher salt
- 1 shallot, thinly sliced
- 1 small jalapeño, seeded and thinly sliced
- 1 2-in. piece peeled fresh ginger, very thinly sliced and cut into matchsticks
- 1 lb cooked peeled and deveined shrimp, tails removed
- 1 avocado, cut into chunks
- ½ 14-oz can hearts of palm, rinsed and sliced
- 1 mandarin orange, cut into segments
- 2 cups mixed fresh herbs (we like cilantro and basil), large leaves torn
- Olive oil, for drizzling
- Plantain chips, for serving

DIRECTIONS

1. In large bowl, whisk together citrus juices, honey and ¾ tsp salt. Stir in shallot, jalapeño and ginger. Toss with shrimp and let sit, tossing occasionally, at least 15 min. and up to 25 min.

2. Fold avocado, palm hearts and citrus segments into shrimp mixture, then gently fold in herbs. Drizzle with oil if desired and serve with chips.

Lunch

Peach Caprese Salad

PER SERVING
~325 cal, 28 g fat (11 g sat), 14 g pro, 135 mg sodium, 9 g carb, 2 g fiber

Fruit is essential to any low-calorie plan. But if you've had enough of the raw stuff, try the grill. It imparts an even sweeter bite to the peaches in this seasonal salad.

ACTIVE TIME 15 min.   **TOTAL TIME** 15 min.   **YIELDS** 4-6 servings

INGREDIENTS

- 2 peaches, each cut into 8 wedges
- 2 Tbsp plus 2 tsp olive oil
- 1½ Tbsp lemon juice
- 1 tsp honey
- Kosher salt and pepper
- 1 tsp grated Meyer lemon zest
- ¼ cup roasted almonds, chopped
- 12 oz fresh mozzarella, sliced
- ¼ cup fresh basil, torn, plus small leaves, for topping

DIRECTIONS

1. Heat grill to medium-high. Brush peaches with 2 tsp oil and grill until grill marks appear, about 1 min. per side. Transfer to plate and let cool slightly.

2. In small bowl, whisk together lemon juice, honey and ¼ tsp each salt and pepper until honey has dissolved. Whisk in remaining 2 Tbsp olive oil; stir in lemon zest and almonds.

3. Arrange mozzarella slices on platter and top with peaches. Fold basil into almond mixture and spoon over peaches. Sprinkle with cracked pepper and small basil leaves if desired.

Lunch

Warm Roasted Cauliflower & Spinach Salad

Pumpkin pie spice isn't just for the dessert table. The blend of cinnamon, ginger, nutmeg and allspice adds warmth to this easy vegetarian recipe.

PER SERVING
~270 cal,
13 g fat (3 g sat),
13 g pro,
435 mg sodium,
29 g carb, 13 g fiber

ACTIVE TIME 20 min.   **TOTAL TIME** 40 min.   **YIELDS** 4 servings

INGREDIENTS

- 3 Tbsp olive oil
- 1 tsp pumpkin pie spice
- ½ tsp ground cumin
- ½ tsp ground coriander
- Kosher salt
- 1 small shallot, finely chopped
- 1 large head cauliflower (about 2 lbs), cut into small florets
- 1 14-oz can lentils, rinsed
- 3 Tbsp white wine vinegar
- 5 cups baby spinach
- 1 oz pecorino cheese, shaved
- ¼ cup pomegranate seeds

DIRECTIONS

1. Heat oven to 425°F. In small saucepan, warm oil, spices and ½ tsp salt just until hot. In medium bowl, pour half of oil mixture over shallot and set aside.

2. On large rimmed baking sheet, toss cauliflower with remaining oil mixture and roast until golden brown and tender, 20 to 25 min.

3. Add lentils and vinegar to shallot mixture and let sit 5 min. When ready to serve, toss with spinach, pecorino, pomegranate seeds and roasted cauliflower.

Lunch

Spice-Dusted Pork

with Crunchy Vegetable Salad

Loaded with flavor, spice-rubbed pork is mixed with crunchy vegetables for a hearty, gluten-free, protein-powered meal.

**PER SERVING
~285 cal**,
11 g fat (2.5 g sat),
36 g pro,
480 mg sodium,
11 g carb, 4 g fiber

ACTIVE TIME 20 min.   **TOTAL TIME** 35 min.   **YIELDS** 4 servings

INGREDIENTS

- 2 Tbsp olive oil, divided
- 2 small pork tenderloins (about ¾ lb each), cut into 4 equal pieces
- 1 tsp chili powder
- 1 tsp ground coriander
- Kosher salt and pepper
- 1 Tbsp white wine vinegar
- 1 tsp Dijon mustard
- 4 baby turnips, thinly sliced
- 2 stalks celery, thinly sliced
- 2 radishes, thinly sliced
- 1 medium beet, peeled, thinly sliced
- 1 small bulb fennel, thinly sliced
- 1 small head butter lettuce, leaves torn (about 2 cups)

DIRECTIONS

1. Heat 1 Tbsp oil in large skillet on medium. Season pork with chili powder, coriander and ½ tsp each salt and pepper and cook, turning occasionally, until golden brown on all sides and instant-read thermometer inserted in center registers 145°F, 10 to 12 min. total. Transfer to cutting board and let rest at least 5 min. before slicing.

2. Meanwhile, in large bowl, whisk together vinegar, mustard, pinch of salt and remaining Tbsp oil. Fold in vegetables and then lettuce. Serve with pork.

*Took picture
Really good
July 2022*

CHAPTER TWO: LUNCH

Lunch

Blackened Fish Tacos

Super-spiced Cajun seasoning creates bold flavor in a pinch, and it's the secret ingredient in this easy, filling dish.

 *So good!*

PER SERVING
~275 cal,
9 g fat (1.5 g sat),
25 g pro,
300 mg sodium,
25 g carb, 5 g fiber

 *Father's Day 2022*

ACTIVE TIME 15 min.   **TOTAL TIME** 25 min.   **YIELDS** 4 servings

INGREDIENTS

- 1 Tbsp plus 2 tsp olive oil
- 4 Tbsp lime juice
- 1 lb tilapia, cut into 3-in. pieces
- Kosher salt
- 2 Tbsp no-salt-added blackening or Cajun seasoning
- ¼ large pineapple, cut into matchsticks (about 1 cup)
- 1 small red pepper, thinly sliced
- 1 Tbsp grated lime zest
- 2 scallions, sliced into 3-in. matchsticks
- 8 small corn tortillas, warmed
- 4 purple cabbage leaves, halved and thinly sliced
- Sour cream and cilantro, for topping
- Lime wedges, for serving

DIRECTIONS

1. Heat oven to 400°F. Drizzle 2 tsp oil on rimmed baking sheet. Drizzle lime juice over tilapia, season with ½ tsp salt and dip in blackening seasoning. Transfer to baking sheet and cook until opaque throughout, 10 to 12 min.

2. In bowl, toss pineapple and red pepper with lime zest, remaining Tbsp oil and ¼ tsp salt; fold in scallions.

3. Top each tortilla with cabbage, fish, and slaw. Top with sour cream and cilantro and serve with lime wedges if desired.

Lunch

Barley Salad
with Strawberries & Buttermilk Dressing

Thanks to barley, a nutritional powerhouse, plus a bit of dairy, this salad is packed with protein and fiber to keep you feeling full.

PER SERVING
~305 cal,
5.5 g fat (3.5 g sat),
13 g pro,
645 mg sodium,
50 g carb, 10 g fiber

ACTIVE TIME 20 min.   **TOTAL TIME** 20 min.   **YIELDS** 4 servings

INGREDIENTS

- 1 cup quick-cooking pearl barley
- Kosher salt and pepper
- 8 oz peas (fresh or thawed from frozen)
- ¼ cup sour cream
- ¼ cup low-fat buttermilk
- 1 tsp Dijon mustard
- 1 tsp poppy seeds
- 1 small shallot, finely chopped
- 5 oz baby spinach
- 1 lb strawberries, hulled and sliced
- 2 oz Parmesan cheese, shaved

Add steak

DIRECTIONS

1. Cook barley per package directions. Drain and rinse under cold water to cool.

2. Meanwhile, if using fresh peas, bring small pot of water to boil. Add ½ tsp salt, then peas, and cook until just tender, 3 min.; run under cold water to cool.

3. In bowl, whisk together sour cream, buttermilk, mustard, poppy seeds, ½ tsp salt and ¼ tsp pepper; stir in shallot.

4. In large bowl, combine spinach, strawberries, Parmesan, peas and barley, then gently toss with half of dressing. Serve with remaining dressing.

TIP

Quick-cooking barley takes just 10 min., while regular barley simmers for 40 min. But you can speed up regular barley in your pressure cooker: Cook 1 cup barley with 2 cups water on high.

CHAPTER TWO: LUNCH

Lunch

Korean Pineapple Beef Lettuce Wraps

Vitamin C–rich pineapple helps to increase iron absorption from beef in this flavorful low-carb dish.

PER SERVING
~318 cal,
17 g fat (18 g sat),
18 g pro,
589 mg sodium,
23 g carb, 1 g fiber

ACTIVE TIME 20 min. **TOTAL TIME** 20 min. **YIELDS** 6 servings

INGREDIENTS

- ½ cup pineapple juice
- 1 clove garlic, grated
- 2 Tbsp low-sodium soy sauce
- ½ tsp red pepper flakes
- 1 Tbsp grated fresh ginger
- 1 Tbsp honey
- 1 Tbsp toasted sesame oil
- 1 lb sirloin, strip steak, or boneless short rib, frozen until just solid (45 to 60 min.)
- 2 Tbsp canola oil
- Kosher salt
- 3 cups cooked sticky rice
- Lettuce leaves, scallions, red chiles and chopped peanuts for serving

DIRECTIONS

1. In medium bowl, combine pineapple juice, garlic, soy sauce, red pepper flakes, ginger, honey and sesame oil. Thinly slice frozen meat, add to marinade and toss to coat. Let marinate 30 min. or cover and refrigerate up to 3 hr. Remove from refrigerator 30 min. before cooking.

2. Heat large stainless steel skillet on medium-high. Add 1 Tbsp canola oil. Transfer half of beef mixture to skillet, arrange in even layer, season with ¼ tsp salt and cook without moving until lightly browned, 1 min. Toss beef and continue to cook until just cooked through and crisp at edges, 2 min. Transfer to plate. Repeat with remaining Tbsp oil and beef.

3. Serve immediately with sticky rice, lettuce leaves, scallions, chiles and peanuts, if desired.

Lunch

Roasted Asparagus & Ricotta Tart

PER SERVING
~205 cal, 14 g fat (5 g sat), 7 g pro, 250 mg sodium, 13 g carb, 1 g fiber

Nestled neatly on a sheet of puff pastry, this tart makes dividing equal portions of veggies for the week ahead a snap. A medley of herbs gives it a burst of fresh flavor.

ACTIVE TIME 10 min.   **TOTAL TIME** 30 min.   **YIELDS** 8 servings

INGREDIENTS

- 1 sheet frozen puff pastry (half of 17.3-oz package), thawed
- 1 large egg, beaten
- 1 cup ricotta cheese
- Kosher salt and pepper
- Zest of 1 lemon
- 2 scallions, chopped
- ¼ cup fresh flat-leaf parsley, chopped
- 1 Tbsp fresh tarragon, chopped
- 12 oz asparagus, trimmed, halved
- ½ Tbsp olive oil

DIRECTIONS

1. Heat oven to 425°F; place oven rack in lower third of oven. Unfold pastry onto piece of parchment paper and roll ½ in. bigger on all sides. Slide parchment and pastry onto baking sheet. In medium bowl, beat egg. Lightly brush ½-in. border of egg around pastry.

2. Add ricotta and ¼ tsp each salt and pepper to bowl with remaining egg. Finely grate zest of lemon into bowl, then fold in scallions and herbs. Spread onto pastry, leaving border uncovered.

3. Top filling with asparagus; drizzle with oil. Bake until crust is golden brown, 18 to 20 min.

CHAPTER TWO: LUNCH

Lunch

Grilled Lamb & Artichoke Kebabs

Instead of dousing your kebabs in a heavy sauce, try the grilled lemon trick in this dish. It enhances the taste with nothing but the heat of the flame.

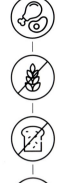

PER SERVING
~265 cal,
14.5 g fat (3.5 g sat),
28 g pro,
320 mg sodium,
8 g carb, 2 g fiber

ACTIVE TIME 25 min. **TOTAL TIME** 1 hr. 30 min. **YIELDS** 8 servings

INGREDIENTS

- 2½ lbs boneless lamb leg, trimmed and cut into 1-in. chunks
- 2 Tbsp olive oil
- 1 tsp ground coriander
- 1 tsp dried oregano
- Kosher salt and pepper
- 3 lemons
- 2 cloves garlic, finely chopped
- ¼ cup flat-leaf parsley, chopped
- 16 large marinated artichoke hearts
- 2 bunches scallions

DIRECTIONS

1. In large bowl, toss lamb with oil, then coriander, oregano and ½ tsp each salt and pepper. Finely grate zest of 2 lemons over lamb; add garlic and parsley and toss to combine. Let sit 1 hr. or refrigerate overnight.

2. Meanwhile, cut all lemons and artichokes in half and scallions crosswise into 2½-in. pieces.

3. Heat grill or grill pan on medium-high. Thread artichokes, scallions and lamb onto skewers.

4. Grill kebabs, turning occasionally, until lamb reaches desired doneness, 6 to 8 min. for medium-rare. Grill lemons, cut sides down, until charred, 2 to 3 min. Squeeze over kebabs.

Lunch

Savory Stone Fruit Soup

This one-pot gazpacho puts a savory twist on your favorite summer fruits by blending them with garlic and sherry vinegar.

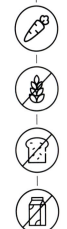

PER SERVING
~175 cal,
11 g fat (1.5 g sat),
2.5 g pro,
245 mg sodium,
20 g carb, 4 g fiber

ACTIVE TIME 10 min.   **TOTAL TIME** 40 min.   **YIELDS** 4 servings

INGREDIENTS

- 1¼ lbs nectarines or peaches (about 4 small), pitted, plus slices for topping
- 1 lb red or orange heirloom tomatoes (about 3), quartered
- 2 Tbsp olive oil, plus more for topping
- 2 tsp sherry vinegar
- 1 small clove garlic, grated
- Kosher salt and pepper

DIRECTIONS

1. In blender, puree nectarines, tomatoes, oil, vinegar, garlic and ½ tsp each salt and pepper until smooth.

2. Refrigerate at least 1 hr. and up to overnight before serving. Serve topped with sliced nectarines, cracked pepper and extra drizzle of oil.

CHAPTER TWO: LUNCH

Lunch

White Bean & Kale Toasts

PER SERVING
~275 cal, 10.5 g fat (2 g sat), 13 g pro, 360 mg sodium, 32 g carb, 10 g fiber

An alternative to hummus, this mix of white beans and garlic creates a creamy, flavorful toast topper. Add the egg for a perfectly well-rounded meal.

ACTIVE TIME 20 min. **TOTAL TIME** 20 min. **YIELDS** 4 servings

INGREDIENTS

- 2 Tbsp olive oil
- 1 yellow onion, thinly sliced
- 2 cloves garlic, thinly sliced
- 1 15-oz can white beans, rinsed
- 3 cups baby kale
- Kosher salt and pepper
- 4½-in.-long sliced baguette, toasted
- 2 hard-boiled eggs, finely grated
- 4 tsp finely grated Parmesan cheese

DIRECTIONS

1. In large skillet, heat oil on medium. Add onion and garlic and sauté until very tender, about 6 min. Add beans and ⅓ cup water and heat through.

2. Add kale, season with salt and pepper and toss until just beginning to wilt, 2 min. Top baguette slices with bean mixture, then eggs and Parmesan.

Lunch

Roasted Red Pepper Soup

Roasted red peppers are a great source of vitamin C, and they also add depth of flavor to this easy fiber-rich soup. Make ahead and store in the freezer to enjoy on a cold autumn or winter day.

PER SERVING
~250 cal,
10 g fat (1.5 g sat),
10 g pro,
700 mg sodium,
32 g carb, 9 g fiber

ACTIVE TIME 20 min. **TOTAL TIME** 30 min. **YIELDS** 4 servings

INGREDIENTS

- 2 Tbsp olive oil
- 1 large onion, chopped
- 4 cloves garlic, smashed
- Kosher salt and pepper
- 1 tsp ground coriander
- 2 12-oz jars roasted red peppers, drained and coarsely chopped
- 1 15-oz can chickpeas, rinsed
- 1 32-oz container low-sodium chicken or vegetable broth
- 2 Tbsp sherry vinegar
- Toasted sliced almonds, sliced scallions and chopped cilantro, for serving

DIRECTIONS

1. Heat large Dutch oven on medium. Add oil, then onion and garlic; season with ½ tsp each salt and pepper and cook, covered, stirring occasionally, 5 min.

2. Uncover, stir in coriander and cook 1 min. Add red peppers, chickpeas and broth; cover and bring to boil. Boil 5 min., then remove from heat and stir in vinegar.

3. Using immersion blender (or standard blender, in batches), puree soup until very smooth. Serve topped with almonds, scallions and cilantro if desired.

TIP

Double or triple the recipe, then freeze in pint- or quart-sized containers for up to 2 months. Thaw in refrigerator overnight then warm in saucepan over medium heat until heated through. Top with almonds, scallions and cilantro before serving.

Lunch

Broccoli "Steaks"
with Spicy Tomato Jam

A Meatless Monday dish that will turn carnivores into veggie lovers, this broccoli-based meal has enough bite to curb midday hunger.

PER SERVING
~265 cal, 10.5 g fat (2.5 g sat), 10 g pro, 595 mg sodium, 36 g carb, 4 g fiber

ACTIVE TIME 30 min.   **TOTAL TIME** 40 min.   **YIELDS** 4 servings

INGREDIENTS

- 1 pint cherry tomatoes
- ¼ cup sugar
- ½ tsp chili powder
- 3½ oz roughly torn baguette (generous 2 cups)
- 1½ oz finely grated Parmesan cheese
- 2 Tbsp olive oil
- 2 broccoli crowns, each cut in half
- Kosher salt and pepper

DIRECTIONS

1. Heat oven to 425°F. In small saucepan, simmer tomatoes, sugar, chili powder and ½ cup water until completely broken down and glossy, 20 to 25 min.

2. In food processor, pulse bread with Parmesan to form coarse crumbs. Spread on rimmed baking sheet and roast until golden brown, 4 to 5 min.

3. Heat large cast-iron skillet on medium-high. Add oil, then broccoli crowns, cut sides down, and cook until golden brown, 5 to 6 min. Flip broccoli, season with ½ tsp each salt and pepper, transfer to oven and roast until just tender, about 16 min. Serve broccoli steak with tomato jam and crumbs.

Lunch

Cucumber-Melon Soup

Looking to cool off from the summer heat? This no-cook soup is refreshing and bright—plus, it comes together entirely in your blender.

PER SERVING
~75 cal,
0 g fat (0 g sat),
3 g pro,
270 mg sodium,
18 g carb, 3 g fiber

ACTIVE TIME 15 min. **TOTAL TIME** 45 min. **YIELDS** 4 servings

INGREDIENTS

- 1 lb English cucumbers, cut into pieces, plus more for topping
- ½ small honeydew melon, seeded and rind removed (about 1 pound), cut into pieces
- ½ cup flat-leaf parsley
- 3 Tbsp red wine vinegar
- 1 Tbsp fresh lime juice
- 2 tsp sugar
- Kosher salt and pepper
- Watercress, for topping

DIRECTIONS

1. In blender, puree cucumbers, melon, parsley, vinegar, lime juice, sugar and ½ tsp salt until smooth.
2. Refrigerate at least 1 hr. or overnight. Serve topped with watercress, sliced cucumber and cracked pepper.

Lunch

Chilled Corn Soup

Soup is a low-calorie winter staple, but you don't have to take it off the menu come summer. This chilled version has just 165 calories per serving and requires minimal prep time.

PER SERVING
~165 cal,
4 g fat (1.5 g sat),
7 g pro,
330 mg sodium,
32 g carb, 4 g fiber

ACTIVE TIME 15 min.   **TOTAL TIME** 15 min.   **YIELDS** 4 servings

INGREDIENTS

- 4 large ears corn, shucked
- ¼ yellow pepper
- ½ yellow heirloom tomato (about 5 oz)
- ½ small sweet onion
- 1 Tbsp fresh lime juice
- Kosher salt
- Queso fresco, cilantro leaves and cayenne, for serving

DIRECTIONS

1. Bring medium pot of water to boil. Add corn and boil 2 min., then drain and run under cold water to cool.

2. Working over bowl, cut kernels off cobs and use back of knife to scrape any remaining bits of kernels and juices. Discard cobs.

3. Transfer corn to blender along with pepper, tomato, onion, lime juice and ½ tsp salt and puree until smooth. Refrigerate at least 30 min. and up to overnight. Serve topped with crumbled queso fresco, cilantro and pinch cayenne.

CHAPTER TWO: LUNCH

Lunch

Tomato Soup
with Parmesan Crostini

Crostini is just a fancy way of saying toasted bread. We doused ours in Parmesan cheese for the perfect pairing with classic tomato soup.

PER SERVING
~185 cal,
8.5 g fat (1.5 g sat),
6 g pro,
395 mg sodium,
24 g carb, 5 g fiber

ACTIVE TIME 10 min.   **TOTAL TIME** 1 hr. 20 min.   **YIELDS** 4 servings

---

INGREDIENTS

- 2¾ lbs tomatoes
- 8 cloves garlic, smashed
- 1 red onion, thickly sliced
- 2 Tbsp olive oil
- Kosher salt and pepper
- 4 ½-in.-long slices baguette
- 3 Tbsp finely grated Parmesan cheese

DIRECTIONS

1. Heat oven to 325°F. On rimmed baking sheet, toss tomatoes, garlic and onion with oil and ½ tsp each salt and pepper. Roast until tomatoes are tender and juicy and onion is tender, 60 to 70 min. Transfer all vegetables to pot along with 4 cups of water; bring to boil, then in blender or with immersion blender, puree until smooth.

2. Heat oven to broil. Arrange baguette slices on baking sheet, top with Parmesan and broil until melted; serve with soup.

Lunch

Caribbean-Style Fish
with Peppers

Jerk seasoning and peppers bring this recipe to life. The result? Fish with a tropical flair that clocks in under 300 calories.

PER SERVING
~260 cal, 8 g fat (1 g sat), 33 g pro, 485 mg sodium, 12 g carb, 3 g fiber

ACTIVE TIME 30 min.   **TOTAL TIME** 40 min.   **YIELDS** 4 servings

INGREDIENTS

- 1 cod fillet (1½ to 1¾ lbs) or other skinless white fish fillet
- 1 tsp salt-free jerk seasoning
- Kosher salt
- 2 Tbsp olive oil
- 1 clove garlic, pressed
- 3 peppers (green, yellow and red), seeded and thinly sliced
- 1 medium red onion, thinly sliced
- 1 carrot, cut into matchsticks
- 1 Scotch bonnet or habanero chile, seeded and thinly sliced
- ½ tsp allspice
- ¼ cup cider vinegar
- 1 lime, halved
- Cilantro, for topping

DIRECTIONS

1. Heat oven to 400°F. Place cod on rimmed baking sheet lined with nonstick foil, sprinkle with jerk seasoning and ½ tsp salt and roast until opaque throughout, 12 to 15 min.

2. Meanwhile, in large skillet on medium, heat oil and garlic until beginning to sizzle, about 2 min. Add peppers, onion, carrot, chile, allspice and ¼ tsp salt and cook, stirring occasionally, until just tender, 5 to 6 min. Add vinegar and cook until it has evaporated and vegetables are tender, 4 to 5 min. more.

3. Transfer fish and peppers to platter and squeeze lime over top, then sprinkle with cilantro.

JERK SPICE MIX

In bowl, combine ½ tsp **fresh thyme leaves**, ½ tsp **brown sugar**, ¼ tsp **paprika**, ¼ tsp **onion powder**, ¼ tsp **ground allspice**, ¼ tsp **ground cinnamon**, ¼ tsp **chipotle powder**, ¼ tsp **ground nutmeg**, and ¼ tsp **kosher salt**.

Lunch

Jerk Shrimp Wraps
with Mango Slaw

Making your own jerk seasoning lets you control the spice level, so keep testing and adjusting until you get your signature mix. Then use it to give these light and healthy wraps a Caribbean kick.

PER SERVING
~195 cal,
5.5 g fat (1 g sat),
21 g pro,
1,064 mg sodium,
16 g carb, 3 g fiber

ACTIVE TIME 25 min.   **TOTAL TIME** 25 min.   **YIELDS** 4 servings

INGREDIENTS

- 1 lb large peeled and deveined shrimp, tails removed
- Jerk Spice Mix (recipe at left)
- 1 Tbsp fresh lime juice
- 1 tsp red wine vinegar
- 1 tsp agave nectar or honey
- Kosher salt and pepper
- 1 small ripe mango, peeled and diced
- ¼ small jicama, peeled and cut into matchsticks
- ¼ cup finely chopped red onion
- 2 Tbsp canola oil
- 8 leaves butter lettuce
- Fresh cilantro leaves, for serving

DIRECTIONS

1. Make jerk spice mix. In bowl, combine thyme, brown sugar, paprika, onion powder, ground allspice, ground cinnamon, chipotle powder, ground nutmeg and salt.
2. Toss shrimp with jerk spice mix and set aside.
3. In bowl, whisk together lime juice, vinegar, agave, ¼ tsp salt and pinch of pepper. Add mango, jicama and onion and toss to combine.
4. Heat cast-iron skillet over medium-high heat. Add oil and heat for 30 seconds, then add shrimp and cook until golden brown and opaque throughout, 4 to 5 min.
5. Divide shrimp among lettuce leaves and top with slaw and cilantro, if using.

Lunch

Sheet Pan Chicken Fajitas

Skinless chicken breast is the perfect low-calorie canvas for a splash of flavor. Here, pineapple adds a sweet twist to an otherwise savory dish.

PER SERVING
~402 cal, 13 g fat (3 g sat), 41 g pro, 490 mg sodium, 30 g carb, 2 g fiber

ACTIVE TIME 20 min.   **TOTAL TIME** 40 min.   **YIELDS** 4 servings

INGREDIENTS

- 4 6-oz boneless, skinless chicken breasts
- 2 Tbsp adobo sauce
-    Kosher salt
- 2 peppers (red and yellow), sliced
- 1 onion, sliced
- ½ small pineapple, cut into matchsticks
- 1 Tbsp olive oil
- 4 tortillas
-    Lime wedges, for serving

DIRECTIONS

1. Heat broiler. Toss chicken breasts with adobo sauce and ¼ tsp salt. Place on rimmed baking sheet and broil 6 min.; transfer to plate. Lower oven temp to 425°F.

2. On same baking sheet, toss peppers, onion and pineapple with olive oil and ¼ tsp salt. Roast 15 min.

3. Nestle chicken amid vegetables and roast until chicken is cooked through and vegetables are tender, 5 min. more. Slice chicken and serve with vegetables, tortillas and lime wedges.

Lunch

Chicken & Avocado Salad Arepas

Zesty lime and spicy jalapeño combined with avocado and chicken create the perfect filling for these gluten-free South American-style sandwiches.

Salad,
PER SERVING
~165 cal,
16 g fat (3 g sat),
7 g pro,
300 mg sodium,
6 g carb, 4 g fiber

Arepas,
PER SERVING
~160 cal,
4.5 g fat (0.5 g sat),
2 g pro,
480 mg sodium,
28 g carb, 1 g fiber

ACTIVE TIME 35 min.   **TOTAL TIME** 50 min.   **YIELDS** 8 servings

INGREDIENTS

- 2 cups precooked cornmeal (masarepa, not masa harina)
- Kosher salt
- 2 Tbsp canola oil
- Chicken and Avocado Salad (recipe below)

DIRECTIONS

1. In large bowl, combine cornmeal and 2 tsp salt. Add 2½ cups warm water and whisk to remove lumps, then stir with spatula to combine. Let rest 5 min. Divide dough into 8 balls and flatten each into 3-in. disk about ½ in. thick.

2. Heat 1 Tbsp oil in large nonstick skillet on medium. In 2 batches, cook 4 arepas, covered, until golden brown on one side, 6 to 8 min. Uncover, flip and cook until other side is golden brown, 5 to 7 min. more.

3. Transfer to wire rack and repeat with remaining oil and arepas. Split and stuff with Chicken and Avocado Salad.

CHICKEN & AVOCADO SALAD

In bowl, mash 2 ripe **avocados** (about 2 cups) with 3 Tbsp **mayonnaise**, 2 Tbsp fresh **lime juice** and ½ tsp **salt**. Add 2 cups shredded **rotisserie chicken** and gently toss to coat, then fold in 2 finely chopped **scallions**, ½ **jalapeño**, seeded and finely chopped, and ¼ cup **cilantro**. Serves 8.

Lunch

Chicken Roulades
with Marinated Tomatoes

Don't let the name scare you—this tenderized chicken is easy to prepare and it turns your ordinary chicken breast into a dinner party-worthy dish.

PER SERVING
~310 cal,
16.5 g fat (4 g sat),
31 g pro,
755 mg sodium,
10 g carb, 3 g fiber

ACTIVE TIME 35 min. **TOTAL TIME** 35 min. **YIELDS** 4 servings

INGREDIENTS

- 4 boneless, skinless chicken breasts
- 2 cloves garlic, finely grated
- 2 Tbsp lemon zest
- ½ cup finely grated Parmesan cheese
- 32 baby spinach leaves
- Kosher salt and pepper
- 3 Tbsp olive oil, divided
- 2 Tbsp lemon juice
- 2 pints grape or cherry tomatoes, sliced
- ¼ small red onion, thinly sliced
- 2 Tbsp red wine vinegar

DIRECTIONS

1. Heat oven to 450°F. Pound chicken breasts into ¼-in thick cutlets. In small bowl, combine garlic, lemon zest and Parmesan. Lay 8 spinach leaves on each cutlet, then sprinkle garlic mixture on top. Roll chicken up and secure with toothpick (insert toothpick parallel to seam to make turning roulades easier). Season chicken with ½ tsp each salt and pepper.

2. In large ovenproof skillet on medium-high, heat 1 Tbsp oil. Carefully add roulades, seam side down, and cook, turning until browned on all sides, 6 to 7 min. Transfer to oven and bake until cooked through, 8 to 9 min. more. Drizzle lemon juice on roulades.

3. While chicken roasts, toss together tomatoes, onion, red wine vinegar, remaining 2 Tbsp oil and ½ tsp each salt and pepper. Serve with chicken.

CHAPTER TWO: LUNCH

Chapter Three
Dinner

Five-Spice Beef Stew
p. 193

Dinner

Seafood, Chorizo & Vegetable Stew

A combination of chorizo and seafood provides this stew with Spanish-inspired flavors and a double dose of hearty protein. The addition of white wine brings depth and complexity.

PER SERVING
~280 cal, 10 g fat (3 g sat), 29 g pro, 1,025 mg sodium, 16 g carb, 4 g fiber

ACTIVE TIME 15 min. **TOTAL TIME** 20 min. **YIELDS** 4 servings

INGREDIENTS

- 1 Tbsp olive oil
- 2 oz Spanish (cured) chorizo, thinly sliced
- 2 stalks celery, thinly sliced
- 1 bulb fennel, cored and thinly sliced
- 2 cloves garlic, thinly sliced
- 1 28-oz can whole peeled tomatoes in juice
- ¾ cup dry white wine
- 1 12-oz cod fillet, cut into 2-in. pieces
- ½ lb large peeled and deveined shrimp
- 1 Tbsp red wine vinegar
- 1 Tbsp fresh tarragon, chopped

DIRECTIONS

1. Heat oil in large pot or Dutch oven over medium-high. Add chorizo and cook, stirring, for 1 min.
2. Add celery, fennel and garlic and cook, covered, stirring occasionally, until beginning to soften, 3 to 4 min.
3. Crush tomatoes and add to pan along with their juices. Add wine and bring to boil. Add cod and shrimp and cook, covered, stirring once, until opaque throughout, 3 to 4 min. Remove from heat and stir in vinegar and tarragon.

Dinner

Mushroom & Brussels Sprouts Pizza

PER SERVING
~485 cal,
19.5 g fat (7 g sat),
16 g pro,
1,360 mg sodium,
58 g carb, 4 g fiber

Make your next pizza party a little lighter by baking your own pie at home. Balsamic-coated vegetables steal the show, so you won't need much cheese to top it all off.

ACTIVE TIME 15 min. **TOTAL TIME** 25 min. **YIELDS** 4 servings

INGREDIENTS

- Cornmeal, for baking sheet
- Flour, for surface
- 1 lb refrigerated (or thawed from frozen) pizza dough
- 3 oz fontina cheese, coarsely grated, divided
- 4 oz shiitake mushrooms, stems discarded, torn
- 1½ Tbsp balsamic vinegar
- 4 large Brussels sprouts, trimmed and thinly sliced
- 1 small red onion, sliced
- 2 Tbsp olive oil
- Kosher salt and pepper
- 2 oz fresh goat cheese
- 6 sprigs fresh thyme

Add canned ck

DIRECTIONS

1. Heat oven to 475°F. Sprinkle baking sheet with cornmeal or line with parchment paper. On lightly floured surface, shape pizza dough into large oval. Transfer to prepared sheet and sprinkle with all but ½ cup fontina.

2. In large bowl, toss mushrooms with balsamic vinegar. Add Brussels sprouts (whole leaves and slices) and onion, drizzle with oil and season with ½ tsp each salt and pepper. Toss to combine and scatter over dough.

3. Sprinkle with remaining fontina, then crumble goat cheese over top and sprinkle with thyme. Bake until crust is deep golden brown and vegetables are tender, 10 to 12 min.

TIP
To keep the crust crispy, heat pizza stone (or baking sheet) in oven while building your pizza so dough will begin to cook as it hits the hot surface.

Dinner

Sheet Pan Sausage & Egg Breakfast Bake

PER SERVING
~300 cal,
21 g fat (6.5 g sat),
17 g pro,
485 mg sodium,
10 g carb, 2 g fiber

Eggs are an excellent low-calorie dinner, but if you're craving something extra hearty, a simple scramble can fall flat. This dish is the perfect solution. With high-protein sausage and juicy mushrooms, it's as filling as it is easy.

ACTIVE TIME 15 min.   **TOTAL TIME** 50 min.   **YIELDS** 4 servings

INGREDIENTS

- 4 uncooked breakfast sausages (6 oz total)
- 4 slices bacon
- 8 oz small cremini mushrooms, halved or quartered if large
- 16 Campari or cocktail tomatoes, halved
- 2 cloves garlic, finely chopped
- 1 Tbsp olive oil
- Kosher salt and pepper
- 4 large eggs
- ½ cup flat-leaf parsley, chopped
- Toast, for serving

DIRECTIONS

1. Heat oven to 400°F. On large rimmed baking sheet, roast sausages and bacon, 15 min.

2. In large bowl, toss mushrooms, tomatoes and garlic with oil and pinch each of salt and pepper. Add to baking sheet and roast 10 min.

3. Make wells among vegetables and crack 1 egg into each space; return to oven and roast until meat is cooked through and egg whites are opaque throughout, 8 to 10 min. more.

4. Sprinkle with parsley and serve with toast if desired.

CHAPTER THREE: DINNER

Dinner

Shrimp Curry & Rice

The smallest bit of garlic and ginger goes a long way. Both of these anti-inflammatory ingredients brighten up this high-protein dish. Lower the carbs by swapping out the rice for cauliflower rice.

PER SERVING
~345 cal, 5.5 g fat (1 g sat), 29 g pro, 1,025 mg sodium, 16 g carb, 4 g fiber

ACTIVE TIME 20 min. **TOTAL TIME** 30 min. **YIELDS** 4 servings

INGREDIENTS

- 1 Tbsp olive oil
- 1 large onion, finely chopped
- Kosher salt and pepper
- 1½ Tbsp grated peeled fresh ginger
- 2 cloves garlic, finely chopped
- 1 Tbsp curry powder
- 1 cup long-grain white rice
- 1 lb medium peeled and deveined shrimp
- 1 cup frozen peas, thawed
- 1 cup fresh ~~cilantro~~ chives, chopped
- Lemon wedges, for serving

DIRECTIONS

1. In large skillet on medium, heat oil. Add onion, season with ¼ tsp each salt and pepper and cook, covered, stirring occasionally, until tender, 6 to 8 min. Add ginger and garlic and cook, stirring, 2 min. Add curry powder and cook, stirring, 1 min.

2. Add rice and stir to coat in onion mixture. Stir in 2 cups water and bring to a boil. Reduce heat and simmer, covered, 15 min.

3. Fold shrimp and peas into rice and cook, covered, until shrimp are opaque throughout and rice is tender, 4 to 5 min. more.

4. Remove from heat and fold in cilantro. Serve with lemon wedges if desired.

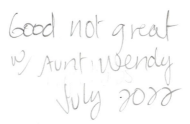

Good not great w/ Aunt Wendy July 2022

CHAPTER THREE: DINNER

Dinner

Orecchiette
with White Beans & Spinach

Beans provide a double dose of hunger-curbing power in the form of protein and fiber. Mix them with your favorite noodles, like we did here, so every bite of pasta packs more good-for-you ingredients.

PER SERVING
~495 cal,
10 g fat (2.5 g sat),
21 g pro,
690 mg sodium,
87 g carb, 8 g fiber

ACTIVE TIME 15 min.   **TOTAL TIME** 20 min.   **YIELDS** 4 servings

INGREDIENTS

- 1 Tbsp olive oil
- 4 cloves garlic, finely chopped
- 2 tsp vegetable bouillon base (we used Better Than Bouillon)
- 12 oz orecchiette or other short pasta
- 2 tsp fresh thyme leaves
- 1 15- to 15.5-oz can small white beans, rinsed
- 3 cups baby spinach
- ½ cup finely grated Parmesan cheese
- Black pepper

DIRECTIONS

1. In large, deep skillet on medium, heat oil and garlic until garlic is light golden brown, about 2 min. Remove from heat, add 4 cups water and whisk in bouillon base.

2. Add orecchiette and thyme and bring to boil. Reduce heat and simmer, stirring frequently, until orecchiette is firm-tender, 10 to 12 min.

3. Fold in beans, spinach, Parmesan and ½ tsp pepper and cook until beans are heated through, about 2 min.

Dinner

Chicken
with Sautéed Apples & Mushrooms

Don't be fooled by the deliciously rich sauce—this one-skillet meal is under 500 calories. Lighter ingredients, like Dijon mustard and shallots, balance out the heavy cream for a high-protein main you'll make again and again.

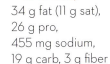

PER SERVING
~475 cal, 34 g fat (11 g sat), 26 g pro, 455 mg sodium, 19 g carb, 3 g fiber

---

ACTIVE TIME 30 min. **TOTAL TIME** 30 min. **YIELDS** 4 servings

INGREDIENTS

- 3 Tbsp olive oil, divided
- 1 10-oz pkg. cremini mushrooms, quartered
- Kosher salt and pepper
- 1 large shallot, finely chopped
- 2 ~~Gala apples, cored and cut into ½-in.-thick wedges~~ Bok Choy
- 1 Tbsp unsalted butter
- 4 chicken thighs (about 1½ lbs)
- ½ cup dry white wine
- ½ cup low-sodium chicken broth
- 6 sprigs thyme, plus more for topping
- ¼ cup heavy cream
- 1 Tbsp Dijon mustard

DIRECTIONS

1. Heat oven to 375°F. Heat 2 Tbsp oil in large oven-safe skillet on medium-high. Add mushrooms and pinch of salt and cook, tossing occasionally, 5 min. Add shallot and cook, stirring occasionally, until mushrooms are golden brown, 2 to 3 min.; transfer to plate. Add apples and butter to skillet and cook, tossing occasionally, until beginning to turn golden brown, 2 to 3 min.; transfer to second plate and wipe skillet clean.

2. Return skillet to medium heat. Rub chicken with remaining Tbsp oil, season with ½ tsp each salt and pepper and cook, skin side down first, until browned, 8 to 10 min; drain excess fat. Turn chicken skin side up, add wine and cook 1 min., then add broth and thyme. Return apples to skillet, transfer skillet to oven and bake until chicken is cooked through (an instant-read thermometer inserted into thickest part should register 165°F), 7 to 8 min.

3. Transfer chicken and apples to plate, discard thyme and return skillet to medium heat. Whisk in cream and mustard, then fold in mushroom mixture and cook until heated through, about 2 min. Serve with chicken and apples and additional thyme if desired.

CHAPTER THREE: DINNER **151**

Dinner

Orange-Ginger Roast Chicken

with Fennel & Radicchio Salad

The combination of citrus and ginger transforms traditional roast chicken into a mouthwatering, full-flavored main.

PER SERVING
~345 cal, 18.5 g fat (5 g sat), 32 g pro, 245 mg sodium, 13 g carb, 3 g fiber

ACTIVE TIME 10 min. **TOTAL TIME** 1 hr. 30 min. **YIELDS** 8 servings

INGREDIENTS

- 2 bulbs fennel, cored and sliced into ¼-in. pieces
- 1 Tbsp olive oil
- Kosher salt and pepper
- 1 navel orange
- 2 Tbsp honey
- 2 Tbsp fresh ginger, grated
- 2 tsp fennel seeds, coarsely crushed
- 1 4- to 5-lbs chicken, giblets discarded, patted dry
- 1 lb mixed mushrooms, cut if large
- 1 Tbsp sherry vinegar
- 1 small head radicchio, torn into large pieces
- Chopped flat-leaf parsley, for serving

DIRECTIONS

1. Heat oven to 350°F. Line rimmed baking sheet with parchment paper. On prepared sheet, toss fennel with oil and ½ tsp each salt and pepper. Move to outer edges of pan.

2. Grate zest of orange into small bowl, then squeeze in 3 Tbsp juice (reserve orange halves). Whisk in honey to dissolve, then stir in ginger and fennel seeds.

3. Place chicken in center of prepared baking sheet and stuff with orange halves, then brush with half of juice mixture. Roast 40 min.

4. Increase oven temp to 425°F. Toss mushrooms with fennel and brush chicken with remaining juice mixture. Roast until instant-read thermometer inserted into thickest part of thigh reads 165°F, 25 to 30 min. Transfer chicken to cutting board and let rest at least 10 min. before carving.

5. Toss mushrooms and fennel with vinegar, season with salt and pepper if necessary and then fold in radicchio. Serve with chicken, topped with parsley if desired.

Dinner

Rotisserie Chicken Cobb Salad

Short on time? This protein-packed, low-carb salad requires minimal prep time and couldn't be easier to toss together.

PER SERVING
~425 cal,
37 g fat (9 g sat),
27 g pro,
955 mg sodium,
12 g carb, 5 g fiber

ACTIVE TIME 15 min. **TOTAL TIME** 20 min. **YIELDS** 4 servings

INGREDIENTS

- 2 Tbsp extra virgin olive oil
- 2 Tbsp red wine vinegar
- Kosher salt and pepper
- 2 plum tomatoes, diced
- 1 rotisserie chicken, shredded (you should have 3 cups)
- 1 avocado, diced
- 4 slices cooked bacon, broken into pieces
- ¼ cup blue cheese, crumbled
- 4 thick slices iceberg lettuce
- 1 hard-cooked egg, grated

DIRECTIONS

1. In large bowl, combine extra virgin olive oil and red wine vinegar with ½ tsp each salt and pepper. Stir in plum tomatoes.

2. Stir chicken into dressing along with avocado, bacon and crumbled blue cheese.

3. Serve over 4 thick slices iceberg lettuce; top with grated hard-cooked egg.

Dinner

Pulled Pork Nachos

Most nachos go heavy on the cheese and light on protein. We added hearty pulled pork and black beans for a zesty dish that will keep you full for hours.

PER SERVING
~330 cal,
15 g fat (6.5 g sat),
23 g pro,
1,565 mg sodium,
26 g carb, 5 g fiber

ACTIVE TIME 20 min.   **TOTAL TIME** 1 hr. 15 min.   **YIELDS** 8 servings

INGREDIENTS

- 3 lbs boneless pork butt, well trimmed and cut into 2-in. pieces (about 2 lbs total)
- 1 tsp ground coriander
- 1 tsp ground cumin
- 1 tsp dried oregano
- Kosher salt and pepper
- 6 cloves garlic, smashed
- 2 jalapeños, halved and seeded
- ¼ cup fresh orange juice
- ¼ cup plus 3 Tbsp fresh lime juice, divided
- ½ small red onion, finely chopped
- 6 oz tortilla chips
- 1 can (15-oz) low-sodium black beans, rinsed
- 6 oz extra-sharp Cheddar, coarsely grated
- 2 plum tomatoes, seeded and cut into ¼-in. pieces
- ½ cup fresh cilantro, chopped
- Sour cream and guacamole, for serving

DIRECTIONS

1. In Instant Pot, toss pork with coriander, cumin, oregano and 1 tsp each salt and pepper. Toss in garlic and jalapeños, then pour orange juice and ¼ cup lime juice over top.

2. Cover and lock lid, then cook on high pressure for 40 min. Use quick-release method to release pressure. Using slotted spoon, transfer pork to large bowl, discarding garlic and jalapeños. Shred meat, then pour 1 cup cooking liquid over top and toss to combine, adding more if meat seems dry.

3. While pork is cooking, toss onion with remaining 3 Tbsp lime juice and ½ tsp each salt and pepper. Let sit, tossing occasionally, until ready to use.

4. Heat oven to 450°F. On large rimmed baking sheet, toss tortilla chips and black beans with half of Cheddar. Sprinkle with 2 cups pork (save rest for another use) then remaining cheese and bake until cheese has melted, about 7 min.

5. Meanwhile, toss tomatoes with onion and fold in cilantro. Spoon over nachos along with sour cream and guacamole.

Dinner

Chicken Mole

Reach for this recipe next time you're in a chicken rut. The combo of homemade hazelnut spread and prepared salsa creates layers of sweet and savory flavor without bumping this dish over 400 calories per serving.

Chicken Mole, PER SERVING
~355 cal, 17.5 g fat (4.5 g sat), 25 g pro, 1,015 mg sodium, 26 g carb, 4 g fiber

Hazelnut Spread, PER SERVING
~80 cal, 4.5 g fat (1.5 g sat), 2 g pro, 45 mg sodium, 8 g carb, 1 g fiber

---

ACTIVE TIME 15 min.   **TOTAL TIME** 45 min.   **YIELDS** 4 servings

INGREDIENTS

- 1 Tbsp olive oil
- 1 large onion, chopped
- 3 cloves garlic, finely chopped
- 2 tsp chili powder
- 1 cup prepared salsa
- 1 cup chicken broth
- ½ cup Homemade Hazelnut Spread (recipe below)
- 2 lbs dark-meat chicken pieces, skin removed
- Kosher salt
- Cooked yellow rice, for serving
- Sesame seeds and sliced scallions, for topping

DIRECTIONS

1. Heat oil in Dutch oven on medium. Add onion, garlic and chili powder and cook until softened, stirring often, about 7 min.

2. Stir in salsa and chicken broth, then whisk in Homemade Hazelnut Spread.

3. Season chicken with ½ tsp salt and add to pot. Simmer until chicken is tender and cooked through, about 30 min. Serve with yellow rice and sprinkle with sesame seeds and scallions if desired.

HOMEMADE HAZELNUT SPREAD

Heat oven to 375°F. Place 1 cup **hazelnuts** on a rimmed baking sheet and roast 10 min., shaking once or twice. Wrap hot hazelnuts in kitchen towel and roll vigorously to remove most of peel; cool completely. In a food processor, process hazelnuts and ½ tsp **kosher salt** until mostly smooth and runny, about 8 min., stopping and scraping the side of the bowl occasionally. In a medium bowl, microwave 3½ oz **dark chocolate**, chopped, in 20-second intervals, stirring after each until melted, then stir in 1 cup **sweetened condensed milk** and 2 Tbsp **light corn syrup**. Add chocolate mixture to pureed hazelnuts; pulse until just combined. Store in airtight container at room temp up to 2 weeks.

Dinner

Greek Lemon Chicken Soup

PER SERVING
~440 cal,
13 g fat (3.5 g sat),
52 g pro,
1,260 mg sodium,
26 g carb, 0 g fiber

This healthy chicken soup recipe will warm you from the inside out! With 52 grams of protein, it's heartier than it looks.

ACTIVE TIME 25 min. **TOTAL TIME** 45 min. **YIELDS** 4 servings

INGREDIENTS

- 1 medium onion, quartered
- 1 leek, white and light green parts only, cut into 1-in. pieces
- 1 stalk celery, cut into 1-in. pieces
- 3 Tbsp low-sodium chicken bouillon base (we used Better than Bouillon)
- 1 bone-in chicken breast (about 2½ lbs), split
- 1 small sprig fresh oregano
- ½ small bunch dill, plus sprigs, for topping
- ½ cup long-grain white rice
- 2 large eggs
- 6 Tbsp fresh lemon juice
- Cracked pepper, for topping

DIRECTIONS

1. In large pot, combine onion, leek, celery and bouillon with 10 cups water and bring to a boil. Reduce heat, add chicken, oregano and dill, and simmer until chicken is just cooked through, 15 to 20 min.

2. Transfer chicken to bowl and when cool enough to handle, shred meat, discarding skin and bones.

3. Strain liquid and return it to pot. Add rice and simmer for 12 min.

4. Meanwhile, in medium bowl, whisk together eggs and lemon juice until foamy and combined.

5. Ladle 1 cup of hot broth from top of soup into measuring cup. Slowly whisk broth, 1 Tbsp at a time, into egg mixture. Then, whisking constantly, gradually add this egg-broth mixture to pot. Simmer until soup is slightly thickened and velvety and rice is tender, about 5 min. Remove from heat; stir in shredded chicken. Serve topped with dill and pepper.

Dinner

Roast Lamb

Lamb is a versatile lean protein. In this uncomplicated and comforting take, you don't need much more than rosemary, thyme, garlic and parsley to bring out all the flavor.

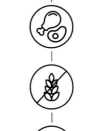

PER SERVING
~320 cal, 22 g fat (8 g sat), 23 g pro, 480 mg sodium, 12 g carb, 2 g fiber

ACTIVE TIME 15 min.   **TOTAL TIME** 45 min.   **YIELDS** 6 servings

INGREDIENTS

- 1 lamb top round (1¼ to 1½ lbs), trimmed
- Kosher salt and pepper
- 12 cloves garlic (4 cloves chopped)
- 1 Tbsp chopped rosemary
- 2 tsp thyme leaves
- 2 Tbsp olive oil, divided
- 2 pints grape tomatoes
- Chopped parsley, for topping

DIRECTIONS

1. Heat oven to 400°F. Season lamb with 1 tsp salt and ½ tsp pepper and place in roasting pan.

2. In small bowl, combine chopped garlic, rosemary, thyme and 1 Tbsp oil. Rub over lamb and roast 10 min.

3. Toss tomatoes and garlic cloves with remaining Tbsp oil and ¼ tsp each salt and pepper. Scatter tomatoes and garlic around lamb and roast until internal temperature of lamb registers 125°F for medium-rare, 15 to 20 min. more. Transfer lamb to cutting board and let rest at least 10 min. before slicing. Serve with tomatoes and garlic and sprinkle with parsley if desired.

Dinner

Beef & Broccoli

A lighter version of the takeout favorite, this crowd-pleaser still has all the flavor of delivery thanks to a combo of fresh ginger, garlic, lime juice and a soy sauce.

PER SERVING
~370 cal,
19.5 g fat (6.5 g sat),
29 g pro,
905 mg sodium,
21 g carb, 4 g fiber

ACTIVE TIME 30 min. **TOTAL TIME** 30 min. **YIELDS** 4 servings

INGREDIENTS

- ⅓ cup low-sodium soy sauce, divided
- 2 Tbsp fresh lime juice
- 2 Tbsp packed brown sugar
- 2 cloves garlic, grated
- 1 Tbsp grated fresh ginger
- 1–2 tsp sriracha
- 1 tsp toasted sesame oil
- 3 tsp cornstarch, divided
- 1 lb sirloin or strip steak, steak halved lengthwise, then thinly sliced
- 1 large head broccoli (about 1 lb), cut into small florets, stem peeled (if necessary) and sliced
- 1 Tbsp canola oil
- White rice, sliced red chiles, sesame seeds and scallions, for serving

DIRECTIONS

1. In medium bowl, whisk together soy sauce, lime juice, sugar, garlic, ginger, sriracha, sesame oil and 2 tsp cornstarch. Transfer half (about ⅓ cup) to small bowl and whisk in remaining tsp cornstarch and ⅓ cup water; set aside.

2. Add steak to remaining sauce, toss to coat and let sit for 15 min.

3. Meanwhile, heat large skillet on medium. Add ½ cup water and bring to simmer. Add broccoli and cook, covered, until bright green and just barely tender, 4 to 5 min. Transfer broccoli to plate.

4. Wipe out skillet and heat oil on medium-high. Cook steak in single layer in two batches until browned, 2 min. per side. Return first batch of steak to skillet, add sauce and simmer until beginning to thicken, 2 to 3 min. Add broccoli and toss to combine.

5. Serve over rice; sprinkle with scallions and sesame seeds, if desired.

CHAPTER THREE: DINNER

Dinner

Summer Squash Pizza

Prepping pizza at home is surprisingly easy with store-bought dough. This version spotlights summer favorites zucchini, yellow squash, fresh herbs and goat cheese.

PER SERVING
~425 cal,
18.5 g fat (5.5 g sat),
12 g pro,
470 mg sodium,
54 g carb, 2 g fiber

ACTIVE TIME 20 min.   **TOTAL TIME** 20 min.   **YIELDS** 4 servings

INGREDIENTS

- 1 small zucchini, halved lengthwise
- ½ small yellow summer squash
- 1 Tbsp plus 4 tsp olive oil, divided, plus more for drizzling
- Kosher salt and pepper
- 1 lb pizza dough, at room temperature
- Flour, for dusting
- ¼ small red onion, thinly sliced
- ½ small red chile, thinly sliced *or Jalapino*
- 2 oz goat cheese, crumbled *or Riccota*
- ½ cup mixed fresh herbs (mint, parsley, chives), chopped

Add canned ck

DIRECTIONS

1. Heat grill to medium-high and arrange so half will give direct heat and other half will give indirect heat.

2. Brush zucchini and squash with 1 Tbsp oil and season with ¼ tsp each salt and pepper. Place vegetables on grill over direct-heat side. Grill, covered, cut side down, until grill marks appear, 3 to 4 min. Flip and grill until barely tender, 1 to 2 min. more; transfer to cutting board and slice.

3. Working on floured surface, shape pizza dough into 12- to 14-in. round and place on flour-dusted baking sheet. Brush top with 2 tsp oil.

4. Transfer pizza dough to grill over direct heat, oiled side down, and grill, covered, until top begins to bubble and bottom is crisp, 2 min. (use tongs to peek underneath).

5. Working quickly, brush top of dough with remaining 2 tsp oil.

6. Flip dough to indirect-heat side of grill, then top with sliced zucchini and squash, onion, chile and goat cheese and continue grilling, covered, until dough is cooked through and charred in spots on bottom, 3 to 5 min. more (cheese will melt during this time).

7. Transfer to cutting board, drizzle with oil and sprinkle with herbs.

CHAPTER THREE: DINNER

ORANGE-SPIKED CHIMICHURRI

Using a vegetable peeler, remove 2 large strips zest from 1 small **orange**. Finely chop zest and place in a bowl. Squeeze in 2 Tbsp **orange juice**. Add 1 tsp grated **lime zest** and 1 Tbsp **lime juice** along with 2 Tbsp **olive oil**; ½ large **red chile**, seeded and finely chopped; 1 **scallion**, finely chopped; ½ cup **cilantro**, chopped; and ¼ cup **parsley**, chopped; then mix to combine.

Dinner

Marinated Flank Steak
with Grilled Broccoli

Citrus-spiked chimichurri adds a South American twist to lean and flavorful flank steak. The vitamin C from the orange and grilled broccoli help to boost iron absorption from the steak.

PER SERVING
~436 cal, 26.5 g fat (10 g sat), 40 g pro, 474 mg sodium, 11 g carb, 4 g fiber

ACTIVE TIME 30 min.   **TOTAL TIME** 55 min. (steak) + 15 min. (broccoli)   **YIELDS** 4 servings

INGREDIENTS

Citrus-Garlic Marinade
- 1½ Tbsp grated orange zest
- 1 Tbsp grated lime zest
- ⅓ cup orange juice
- 2 Tbsp lime juice
- 2 Tbsp olive oil
- 1½ tsp cumin seeds
- 2 cloves garlic, finely chopped

Grilled Broccoli
- 2 Tbsp unsalted butter, at room temperature
- 2 tsp grated lemon zest
- 1 Tbsp lemon juice
- 1 small clove garlic, finely grated
- ½ tsp honey
- ½ small red chile, seeded and finely chopped
- Kosher salt and pepper
- 1½ lbs broccoli crowns, cut lengthwise into 1-in.-thick slices
- 2 Tbsp olive oil

Flank Steak
- 1 lbs flank steak
- Orange-Spiked Chimichurri, for serving (recipe at left)

DIRECTIONS

1. Make marinade: Combine orange zest, lime zest, orange juice, lime juice, olive oil, cumin seeds and garlic in resealable plastic bag. Add steak, seal and turn to coat. Let sit at least 30 min. or refrigerate up to 2 hr.

2. Meanwhile, make broccoli: Heat grill to medium-high. In large bowl, combine butter, lemon zest and juice, garlic, honey, chile and ¼ tsp each salt and pepper.

3. Brush broccoli with oil and season with ½ tsp each salt and pepper. Grill until lightly charred and just barely tender, 2 to 3 min. per side. Transfer to bowl with lemon butter and toss to coat (butter will melt as it is tossed with hot broccoli).

4. Make steak: Heat grill to medium-high. Remove steak from marinade, scraping off any large bits. Season with ½ tsp each salt and pepper and grill, covered, 4 min.

5. Turn and grill, covered, to desired doneness, 3 to 5 min. more for medium-rare (135°F), depending on thickness. Transfer to cutting board and let rest 10 min. before slicing. Serve with Orange-Spiked Chimichurri and broccoli.

Dinner

Shrimp Enchiladas
with Zucchini & Corn

Shrimp is a lean protein that stores well in the freezer and cooks up quickly, making it a low-calorie kitchen staple. Used in this traditional Mexican dish, it adds a juicy, satisfying bite.

PER SERVING
~420 cal, 17 g fat (6 g sat), 26 g pro, 1,745 mg sodium, 42 g carb, 7 g fiber

ACTIVE TIME 25 min.   **TOTAL TIME** 35 min.   **YIELDS** 4 servings

INGREDIENTS

- 1 15-oz jar mild green salsa
- 2 cups fresh cilantro (including stems)
- ¼ cup sour cream
- 1 Tbsp olive oil
- 2 small zucchini (about 8 oz), cut into ¼-in. pieces
- 1 lb peeled and deveined shrimp, cut into ½-in. pieces
- 1 tsp ground coriander
- ½ tsp chili powder
- Kosher salt
- 2 cloves garlic, finely chopped
- 1 cup fresh corn kernels (or frozen corn kernels, thawed)
- ¼ cup grated Cotija cheese
- 8 small yellow corn tortillas
- 2 oz Monterey Jack cheese, coarsely grated
- Chopped red onion and cilantro, sliced radishes and jalapeño, for serving

DIRECTIONS

1. Heat oven to 450°F. In food processor, puree salsa and cilantro until smooth. Add sour cream and pulse to combine. Spread 1 cup mixture in 7- by 11-in. baking dish. Transfer remaining mixture to medium bowl.

2. Heat oil in large skillet on medium-high. Add zucchini and cook 2 min. Add shrimp, then season with coriander, chili powder and ½ tsp salt and cook, tossing, 1 min. Add garlic and cook, tossing, 1 min. Remove from heat and toss with corn and Cotija (shrimp shouldn't be fully cooked).

3. Wrap tortillas in double layer of damp paper towels; microwave on High until soft, about 1 min. (be careful of steam when removing). Working with 1 tortilla at a time, dip in reserved salsa mixture, shaking off any excess. Place on cutting board, top with heaping ¼ cup filling, roll up and place, seam side down, in baking dish. Repeat with remaining tortillas and filling.

4. Spoon any remaining salsa mixture on top. Sprinkle with Monterey Jack and bake until cheese begins to brown, 8 to 10 min. Serve topped with onion, cilantro, radishes and jalapeño.

Dinner

Grilled Fajita Kebabs

An easy and flavorful weeknight meal to put into your regular rotation. A pinch of cayenne adds a touch of heat and a calorie-burning boost.

PER SERVING
~480 cal,
19 g fat (5 g sat),
35 g pro,
1,350 mg sodium,
42 g carb, 5 g fiber

ACTIVE TIME 30 min.   **TOTAL TIME** 30 min.   **YIELDS** 6 servings

INGREDIENTS

- 3 limes
- 1 tsp ground coriander
- ½ tsp ground cumin
- Pinch of cayenne
- 4 Tbsp olive oil, divided
- 1 lb large peeled and deveined shrimp, tails discarded
- 1 lb boneless, skinless chicken breast, cut into 1½-in. pieces
- 1 lb mixed-color peppers, cut into 1-in. pieces
- 3 jalapeños, sliced ½ in. thick
- 2 small red onions, cut into 1-in.-thick wedges
- Kosher salt and pepper
- 12 small flour tortillas
- 6 Tbsp sour cream
- Sliced radishes and chopped cilantro, for serving

DIRECTIONS

1. Finely grate zest of 1 lime into bowl. Add coriander, cumin, cayenne and 2 Tbsp oil and mix to combine. Transfer half to medium bowl and toss with shrimp. In second bowl, toss chicken with remaining mixture.

2. Thread each protein onto its own skewer. Halve all limes.

3. Toss peppers, jalapeños and onions with remaining 2 Tbsp oil and ½ tsp each salt and pepper. Thread jalapeños, peppers and onions onto their own skewers.

4. Heat grill to medium-high. Season chicken and shrimp skewers with ½ tsp each salt and pepper.

5. Add skewers to grill and cook, turning occasionally, until chicken is cooked through (8 to 10 min.), vegetables are just tender (4 to 8 min.) and shrimp is opaque throughout (3 to 4 min.). Transfer skewers to platter as they finish cooking. Grill limes, cut sides down, and tortillas until lightly charred, about 1 min.

6. Squeeze 1 grilled lime half over chicken and shrimp. Serve with vegetables, tortillas, remaining limes, sour cream, radishes and cilantro.

Dinner

Oven-Roasted Salmon
with Charred Lemon Vinaigrette

Swap out your standard salmon recipe for this equally easy, exciting alternative. The charred lemon and mustard add zest to this omega-rich, heart-healthy fish.

PER SERVING
~305 cal, 14 g fat (2.5 g sat), 31 g pro, 400 mg sodium, 14 g carb, 5 g fiber

ACTIVE TIME 15 min.   **TOTAL TIME** 35 min.   **YIELDS** 4 servings

INGREDIENTS

- 1 lemon
- 2 bulbs fennel, thinly sliced
- 2 small red onions, thinly sliced
- 2½ Tbsp olive oil, divided
- Kosher salt and pepper
- 1 lb skin-on salmon fillet
- 1 tsp stone-ground mustard
- 3 cups baby arugula

DIRECTIONS

1. Heat broiler. Cut pointed ends off lemon, halve crosswise, and place on rimmed baking sheet, center cut sides up. Broil on top rack until charred, 5 min.; transfer to plate and set aside.

2. Reduce oven temperature to 400°F. On rimmed baking sheet, toss fennel and onions with 1½ Tbsp oil and ¼ tsp each salt and pepper; arrange around edges of sheet. Place salmon in center of sheet and season with ¼ tsp each salt and pepper. Roast until vegetables are tender and salmon is opaque throughout, 17 to 20 min.

3. Meanwhile, juice charred lemon halves into small bowl and whisk in mustard and remaining Tbsp oil. Remove baking sheet from oven and fold arugula into vegetables. Drizzle charred lemon vinaigrette over fish and vegetables and gently toss vegetables.

TIP

Charring citrus fruits like lemon helps loosen up and release juices while also adding a slight smoky flavor. This method works well on the grill, too—grill the fruit cut side down on medium-high until charred, 1 to 2 min.

Dinner

Cod in Parchment
with Orange-and-Leek Couscous

Cooking in parchment paper steams the fish and veggies for a healthy low-fat meal with easy cleanup!

PER SERVING
~340 cal, 5 g fat (1 g sat), 32 g pro, 330 mg sodium, 40 g carb, 3 g fiber

ACTIVE TIME 15 min.   **TOTAL TIME** 30 min.   **YIELDS** 4 servings

INGREDIENTS

- 1 cup couscous
- 1 orange
- 1 leek, white and light green parts only, cut in half lengthwise, then sliced ½ in. thick
- 3 cups baby kale
- 1¼ lbs cod, cut into 4 portions
- 1 Tbsp olive oil
- Kosher salt and pepper

DIRECTIONS

1. Heat oven to 425°F. Tear off four 12-in. squares of parchment paper and arrange on two baking sheets. In bowl, combine couscous with ¾ cup water.

2. Cut orange in half, then peel one half and coarsely chop fruit. Fold orange into couscous along with leek and baby kale.

3. Divide couscous mixture among pieces of parchment and top each with piece of cod. Drizzle with oil and sprinkle with ½ tsp salt and ¼ tsp pepper, then squeeze remaining orange half over top.

4. Cover each with another piece of parchment and fold each edge up and under three times, tucking edge underneath. Roast 12 min.

5. Transfer each packet to plate. Using scissors or knife, cut an "X" in center and fold back triangles.

Dinner

Bánh Mì

This tongue-tingling pork Bánh mì sandwich gets a hit of spice from hot sauce and jalapeños and plenty of freshness from quick-pickled vegetables. At 400 calories, it proves a stacked sandwich doesn't have to be loaded with calories.

PER SERVING
~400 cal, 15 g fat (2.5 g sat), 24 g pro, 980 mg sodium, 44 g carb, 3 g fiber

ACTIVE TIME 15 min. **TOTAL TIME** 25 min. **YIELDS** 4 servings

INGREDIENTS

- 1 Tbsp olive oil
- 12 oz pork tenderloin, halved
- 1 tsp five-spice powder
- Kosher salt and pepper
- 3 Tbsp maple syrup, divided
- 1 Tbsp fish sauce
- ½ cup rice vinegar
- 2 large carrots, julienned
- 1 4-in. piece daikon radish, peeled with julienne peeler
- 1 jalapeño, thinly sliced
- 2 soft French sandwich rolls or 1 baguette, cut in 4 and split
- 1 cup cilantro
- Mayonnaise and sriracha, for serving

DIRECTIONS

1. Heat oven to 425°F. Heat oil in medium skillet on medium-high. Season pork with five-spice powder and ¼ tsp salt and cook, turning occasionally, until browned on all sides, about 6 min. Transfer skillet to oven and roast until instant-read thermometer inserted into center registers 145°F, 15 to 18 min.

2. Mix 2 Tbsp maple syrup and fish sauce. Spoon maple mixture over pork, then transfer to cutting board and let rest at least 5 min. before slicing.

3. While pork is cooking, make quick pickles: Whisk together vinegar, remaining Tbsp maple syrup and ½ tsp salt to dissolve. Add carrots, radish and jalapeño and let sit, tossing occasionally, until pork is ready.

4. Spread bread with mayonnaise. Pile with pickles and ½ cup cilantro. Top with pork and remaining cilantro and drizzle with sriracha, if desired.

Dinner

Crispy Chicken Thighs
with Buttermilk Fennel Salad

This lower-calorie version of crispy chicken serves as the perfect topper to a fresh greens and fennel salad.

PER SERVING
~450 cal,
27 g fat (8 g sat),
41 g pro,
495 mg sodium,
10 g carb, 4 g fiber

ACTIVE TIME 15 min.   **TOTAL TIME** 35 min.   **YIELDS** 4 servings

INGREDIENTS

- 8 small chicken thighs (about 2½ lbs)
- Kosher salt and pepper
- ¼ cup sour cream
- ¼ cup low-fat buttermilk
- 1½ Tbsp fresh lemon juice
- 1 tsp Dijon mustard
- 1 Tbsp fresh tarragon, chopped
- 6 cups torn lettuce or mixed greens
- 1 medium bulb fennel, cored and thinly sliced
- 1 small seedless cucumber, cut into matchsticks
- 2 scallions, thinly sliced

DIRECTIONS

1. Season chicken with ¼ tsp each salt and pepper and place in large cast-iron skillet, skin side down. Place smaller skillet on top of chicken and put heavy cans in skillet (the contents won't cook) to weigh it down (this will flatten chicken so it cooks up evenly and extra-crisp). Turn heat on medium and cook until skin is deeply browned and crisp, 12 to 14 min. Flip chicken and cook, uncovered, until cooked through, 4 to 5 min. more.

2. Meanwhile, in large bowl, whisk together sour cream, buttermilk, lemon juice, mustard and ¼ tsp each salt and pepper; stir in tarragon.

3. Add lettuce and toss to coat, then fold in fennel, cucumber and scallions. Serve with chicken.

TIP
Stacking a weighted skillet on top of these chicken thighs ensures close contact with the hot skillet for seriously crisp skin.

Dinner

Spring Vegetable Pizza

PER SERVING
~435 cal, 13.5 g fat (5.5 g sat), 16 g pro, 985 mg sodium, 58 g carb, 3 g fiber

Lighten up a homemade pizza with snap peas, leeks and asparagus for the freshest of springtime dinners.

ACTIVE TIME 15 min. **TOTAL TIME** 35 min. **YIELDS** 4 servings

INGREDIENTS

- 1 lb pizza dough, thawed if frozen
- Cornmeal and flour, for dusting
- 4 oz part-skim ricotta cheese
- 4 oz fresh goat cheese, at room temperature
- 1 Tbsp lemon zest
- Kosher salt
- 3 oz asparagus, trimmed and cut into 2-in. pieces
- 3 oz sugar snap peas, strings removed, halved diagonally
- 1 leek (white and light green parts only), thinly sliced into half-moons
- 1 clove garlic, grated
- 1 Tbsp lemon juice
- 2 tsp olive oil

DIRECTIONS

1. Heat oven to 475°F. Let pizza dough stand at room temperature until ready to use.
2. Sprinkle large rimmed baking sheet with cornmeal. In small bowl, combine ricotta, goat cheese, lemon zest and pinch salt.
3. On lightly floured surface, shape pizza dough into large oval or round and place on prepared baking sheet.
4. In large bowl, toss asparagus, snap peas, leek and garlic with lemon juice and oil. Spread ricotta mixture evenly over dough, leaving a ½-in. border all around edges, then top with vegetable mixture. Bake until golden brown and crisp, 13 to 16 min.

Dinner

Pea Fritters
with Shrimp Salad

These fritters only taste indulgent. Made from nutrient-rich peas, they crisp up quickly and will keep you full when paired with shrimp salad. Enjoy them hot or cold.

PER SERVING
~435 cal,
20 g fat (6 g sat),
37 g pro,
1,035 mg sodium,
26 g carb, 5 g fiber

ACTIVE TIME 25 min.   **TOTAL TIME** 30 min.   **YIELDS** 4 servings

INGREDIENTS

- 2 cups frozen (thawed) peas, divided
- 1 large egg plus 1 egg yolk
- 2 Tbsp melted unsalted butter
- Kosher salt and pepper
- ½ cup all-purpose flour
- 2 Tbsp olive oil, divided
- 1 Tbsp mayonnaise
- 2 tsp Dijon mustard
- 1 tsp lemon zest
- 3 Tbsp lemon juice, divided
- ½ small red onion, finely chopped
- 1 lb shrimp, cooked and peeled
- 2 small cucumbers, shaved into ribbons
- 2 cups mixed greens

DIRECTIONS

1. In food processor, pulse 1 cup peas with egg, egg yolk, butter, 1 Tbsp water and 1 tsp salt until coarsely chopped. Fold in flour and remaining peas.

2. Heat 1 Tbsp oil in large nonstick skillet on medium. Drop 4 large spoonfuls batter (about scant ¼ cup each) onto pan, flatten slightly, and cook until golden brown, about 3 min. per side; transfer to plates. Repeat with remaining batter.

3. Meanwhile, in large bowl, whisk together mayonnaise, mustard, lemon zest and 2 Tbsp lemon juice; stir in onion, then toss with shrimp.

4. Toss cucumbers with remaining Tbsp oil, remaining Tbsp lemon juice and ¼ tsp each salt and pepper; toss with greens. Serve with fritters and shrimp.

Dinner

Lemon-Thyme Chicken

This high-protein weeknight dinner is full of good-for-you ingredients. Trust us, you'll want to double the amount of Parmesan-thyme roasted veggies.

PER SERVING
~345 cal, 13.5 g fat (3.5 g sat), 41 g pro, 680 mg sodium, 14 g carb, 3 g fiber

ACTIVE TIME 20 min. **TOTAL TIME** 30 min. **YIELDS** 4 servings

INGREDIENTS

- 1 lb green beans, trimmed
- 12 sprigs fresh thyme, divided
- 2 Tbsp olive oil, divided
- Kosher salt and pepper
- ½ cup grated Parmesan cheese, divided
- 1 14-oz can artichoke hearts, halved and patted very dry
- 1½ lbs boneless, skinless chicken breasts
- 1 lemon, halved

DIRECTIONS

1. Heat oven to 425°F. On rimmed baking sheet, toss green beans and 6 sprigs thyme with 1 Tbsp oil and ¼ tsp each salt and pepper, then toss with ¼ cup Parmesan. Nestle artichokes onto pan, cut sides down, and roast on bottom rack in oven until golden brown and tender, 10 to 12 min.

2. Meanwhile, heat remaining Tbsp oil in large oven-safe skillet on medium. Season chicken with ¼ tsp each salt and pepper and cook until golden brown on bottom, 3 to 4 min. Flip chicken over and cook 2 min. more.

3. Add lemon, cut side down, and remaining 6 thyme sprigs to skillet. Transfer skillet to oven along with vegetables and roast until chicken is cooked through, 9 to 10 min. more.

4. Toss remaining Parmesan with artichokes and green beans, then serve with chicken.

CHAPTER THREE: DINNER

Dinner

Spiced Cod
with Rice Noodle Salad

Cod cooks up in just 5 minutes, making it ideal for busy weeknights. Here it brings a substantial dose of protein to a light and flavorful bed of rice noodles.

PER SERVING
~395 cal,
9 g fat (1 g sat),
22 g pro,
485 mg sodium,
55 g carb, 1 g fiber

ACTIVE TIME 15 min. **TOTAL TIME** 25 min. **YIELDS** 4 servings

INGREDIENTS

- 8 oz rice vermicelli noodles
- 1 cup snow peas, sliced lengthwise
- 3 Tbsp fresh lime juice
- 1 Tbsp fish sauce
- 2 tsp sugar
- ½ red chile, thinly sliced
- 2 Tbsp oil
- 1 Tbsp grated fresh ginger
- ½ tsp ground turmeric
- 1 lb skinless cod fillet, cut into large chunks
- Kosher salt and pepper
- ¼ cup chopped dill
- 1 scallion, thinly sliced
- Chopped peanuts, for topping

DIRECTIONS

1. Cook rice vermicelli noodles per pkg. directions, adding snow peas during last min. of cooking; drain and rinse in cold water.

2. In small bowl, mix lime juice, fish sauce, sugar and 1 tsp water; stir in red chile. Toss half of sauce with noodles and snow peas.

3. In large bowl, mix oil, fresh ginger and ground turmeric. Toss with cod fillet chunks, then season with ¼ tsp each of kosher salt and pepper.

4. Cook fish in large nonstick skillet on medium, turning occasionally, until opaque throughout, 4 to 5 min. Sprinkle with chopped dill and sliced scallion. Serve over noodles with remaining dressing; top with chopped peanuts.

TIP
You could make this dish with any white fish (check thinner fillets after 2 min.) or even shrimp or scallops.

Dinner

Light Chicken Cacciatore

Skip the pasta and bring on the veggies in this healthy chicken dish. You'll save calories but keep the decadent flavor thanks to the rich sauce.

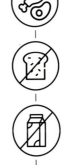

PER SERVING
~300 cal,
10 g fat (1.5 g sat),
36 g pro,
690 mg sodium,
15 g carb, 3 g fiber

ACTIVE TIME 30 min.   **TOTAL TIME** 50 min.   **YIELDS** 6 servings

INGREDIENTS

- 2 Tbsp olive oil
- 6 small boneless, skinless chicken breasts (5 oz each)
- Kosher salt and pepper
- 10 oz cremini mushrooms, quartered
- 1 small onion, thinly sliced
- 1 red pepper, thinly sliced
- 2 cloves garlic, finely chopped
- 2 tsp fresh rosemary, finely chopped
- 1 bay leaf
- ¾ cup dry white wine
- 1 28-oz can diced tomatoes
- 8 oz kale, stems discarded and leaves chopped
- ½ cup pitted green olives
- ¼ cup flat-leaf parsley, chopped

DIRECTIONS

1. Heat oil in large deep skillet on medium-high. Season chicken with ½ tsp each salt and pepper and cook until golden brown, 3 to 4 min. per side; transfer to plate.

2. Add mushrooms to pan and cook, tossing occasionally, until golden brown and tender, about 4 min. Transfer to plate with chicken.

3. Lower heat to medium and add onion, red pepper, garlic, rosemary and bay leaf and cook, stirring occasionally, until tender, 8 to 10 min. Add wine and cook, stirring and scraping up browned bits, until reduced by half, about 3 min. Stir in tomatoes (and their juices).

4. Return chicken and mushrooms to skillet, nestling chicken in tomatoes, and simmer, covered, for 15 min. Fold in kale and cook, covered, 10 to 12 min. more. Uncover, discard bay leaf, and stir in olives and parsley.

Dinner

Five-Spice Beef Stew

Vegetables and spices come together to create an elevated beef stew.

PER SERVING
~365 cal,
12 g fat (2.5 g sat),
41 g pro,
950 mg sodium,
28 g carb, 7 g fiber

ACTIVE TIME 1 hr.   **TOTAL TIME** 2 hr. 30 min.   **YIELDS** 6 servings

INGREDIENTS

- 2 lbs boneless beef bottom round, trimmed and cut into 2-in. chunks
- Kosher salt and pepper
- 2 Tbsp canola or vegetable oil, divided
- 4 cups low-sodium beef broth, divided
- 4 medium shallots, quartered
- 3 cloves garlic, finely chopped
- 1 2-in. piece ginger, finely chopped
- 1 tsp Chinese five-spice powder
- 3 star anise pods
- 1 small cinnamon stick
- 2 Tbsp tomato paste
- 12 oz medium carrots (about 3), peeled and cut into 1-in. pieces
- 12 oz medium parsnips (about 3), peeled and cut into 1-in. pieces
- 2 small purple-topped turnips, cut into 1-in. pieces
- 1 15-oz can crushed tomatoes
- 1 large bunch spinach, thick stems discarded
- 2 Tbsp fish sauce
- 1 Tbsp lime juice
- Cilantro and thinly sliced red chile, for topping

DIRECTIONS

1. Heat oven to 325°F. Season beef with ½ tsp each salt and pepper. Heat 1 Tbsp oil in large Dutch oven on medium-high. Working in batches, cook beef, turning occasionally, until browned, 6 to 8 min. Transfer to bowl; repeat with remaining beef.

2. Add ½ cup broth to pot and cook, scraping up any browned bits, 1 min.; transfer juices to bowl with beef.

3. Lower heat to medium and add remaining 1 Tbsp oil to pot along with shallots and cook, stirring occasionally, until golden brown, 3 to 4 min. Add garlic, ginger, five-spice powder, star anise and cinnamon and cook, stirring, 2 min.

4. Stir in tomato paste and cook 1 min. Return beef and juices to pot along with carrots, parsnips, turnips, tomatoes and remaining 3½ cups broth. Bring to boil, then cover and bake until beef is very tender, 1½ to 2 hr.

5. Remove from oven and discard star anise and cinnamon. Stir in spinach, fish sauce and lime juice. Serve topped with cilantro and chile.

Dinner

Sausage Cauliflower Skillet Cassoulet

PER SERVING
~460 cal,
23 g fat (8 g sat),
22 g pro,
670 mg sodium,
43 g carb, 9 g fiber

Warming, wintry meals don't have to be high in calories. In this one-skillet dish, whole grains, veggies and flavorful sausage offer a satisfying combo of protein and fiber.

ACTIVE TIME 30 min.   **TOTAL TIME** 1 hr.   **YIELDS** 6 servings

INGREDIENTS

- 1 Tbsp plus 1 tsp olive oil, divided
- 12 oz sweet Italian sausages, casings removed
- 3 cloves garlic, finely chopped
- 1 medium onion, finely chopped
- 2 tsp thyme leaves, divided
- 1 cup semi-pearled farro
- ½ large head cauliflower, cored and sliced
- 2 cups low-sodium chicken broth
- 1 15-oz can low-sodium white beans, rinsed
- 1 cup flat-leaf parsley leaves
- Kosher salt and pepper
- ¼ cup panko breadcrumbs
- ⅓ cup finely grated Parmesan cheese

DIRECTIONS

1. Heat 1 Tbsp oil in large cast-iron skillet on medium and cook sausage, breaking up with spoon until browned around edges, 5 to 6 min.

2. Add garlic, onion and 1 tsp thyme; cook, stirring occasionally, 5 min.

3. Add farro, cauliflower and broth and bring to boil. Reduce heat and simmer, stirring occasionally, until farro is tender, 28 to 30 min. Stir in beans, parsley and ¼ tsp each kosher salt and pepper.

4. Heat broiler. Combine panko with remaining tsp oil and thyme, then toss with Parmesan; sprinkle over bean mixture. Broil until golden brown and bubbling around edges, 2 to 3 min.

TOMATO-BASIL SAUCE

Heat large skillet on medium-low and cook 3 Tbsp **olive oil**, 2 cloves sliced **garlic** and 3 **anchovies** until anchovies start to dissolve and garlic starts to turn golden brown, 2 to 3 min. Stir in 3 cups **cherry tomatoes**, halved, and cook until tomatoes just start to break down, 3 to 4 min. Remove from heat and stir in pinch **salt**, ¼ tsp **pepper** and ¼ cup fresh **basil leaves**, torn.

Dinner

Tomato-Basil Gnocchi

Simple, yet so delicious, this recipe includes added protein from the omega-3-rich anchovies in the sauce.

PER SERVING
~335 cal,
18.5 g fat (8 g sat),
14 g pro,
950 mg sodium,
28 g carb, 2 g fiber

ACTIVE TIME 40 min.   **TOTAL TIME** 40 min.   **YIELDS** 6 servings

INGREDIENTS

- 1 lb fresh ricotta cheese
- 1 large egg yolk
- 1¼ cups all-purpose flour, plus more for rolling
- 2 Tbsp freshly grated Parmesan cheese, plus more for topping
- ½ cup fresh basil, roughly chopped
- ¼ tsp ground nutmeg
- Kosher salt and pepper
- Tomato-Basil Sauce (recipe at left)

DIRECTIONS

1. In large bowl, combine ricotta and egg yolk. Add 1 cup flour, Parmesan, basil, nutmeg and ¼ tsp each salt and pepper. Fold together to make a soft but not sticky dough; do not overmix. Add remaining ¼ cup flour as needed.

2. Lightly flour large baking sheet. Divide ricotta mixture into 4 pieces. With lightly floured hands, roll each piece into 1-in.-wide log (about 8 in. long); place on prepared baking sheet and refrigerate, covered loosely with plastic wrap, 30 min.

3. Cut gnocchi logs into 1-in. pieces. Bring large pot of water to boil; add 1 Tbsp salt. Add gnocchi and cook until all have risen to surface, 2 to 3 min., then cook 1 min. more. Using a large slotted spoon, transfer gnocchi to skillet with sauce, gently tossing to coat. Sprinkle with grated Parmesan if desired.

Dinner

Mixed Greens & Herb Toss Salad

PER SERVING
~201 cal, 15 g fat (3 g sat), 11 g pro, 383 mg sodium, 7 g carb, 3 g fiber

The trick to building a salad that will actually fill you up? Layer on the protein. Edamame is a great plant-based source of this satiating macronutrient, with about 17 grams per cup.

ACTIVE TIME 10 min. **TOTAL TIME** 10 min. **YIELDS** 6 servings

INGREDIENTS

- 6 cups mixed spring greens (like Bibb, pea shoots and mâche), torn
- 2 cups mixed herbs (like tarragon, dill, mint and chives), chopped
- 1 cup shelled edamame
- ¼ cup olive oil
- 1 Tbsp lemon juice
- 2 tsp Dijon mustard
- 1 tsp honey
- Kosher salt and pepper
- 1 small shallot, finely chopped
- 6 soft-cooked eggs
- Edible flowers, for serving

DIRECTIONS

1. In large bowl, toss greens and herbs. Fold in edamame.
2. In bowl, whisk together olive oil, lemon juice, mustard, honey and ¼ tsp each salt and pepper; stir in shallot.
3. Gently toss salad with dressing and top with eggs and flowers, if desired.

CHAPTER THREE: DINNER

Dinner

Herbed Ricotta & Fresh Tomato Tart

PER SERVING
~300 cal, 21 g fat (9.5 g sat), 10 g pro, 280 mg sodium, 25 g carb, 2 g fiber

Celebrate the best flavors of summer with juicy tomatoes, fresh parsley and mint combined with creamy ricotta.

ACTIVE TIME 15 min. **TOTAL TIME** 40 min. **YIELDS** 6 servings

INGREDIENTS

- 1 sheet frozen puff pastry (from 17.3-oz pkg.), thawed
- 1 large egg, beaten
- 1 cup ricotta cheese
- Kosher salt and pepper
- 1 lemon
- 2 scallions, finely chopped
- ½ cup fresh flat-leaf parsley, chopped
- 1 lb heirloom tomatoes (various colors and sizes), sliced or halved
- 2 Tbsp olive oil
- ¼ cup small fresh mint leaves
- Flaky sea salt, for topping

DIRECTIONS

1. Heat oven to 425°F and place oven rack in lower third of oven. Unfold pastry onto piece of parchment paper and roll ½ in. bigger on all sides. Slide parchment (and pastry) onto baking sheet.

2. Using paring knife, score ½-in. border all around pastry. Lightly brush border with egg. Using fork, poke middle of pastry all over, then bake until golden brown, 20 to 25 min.

3. Meanwhile, in medium bowl, combine ricotta and ¼ tsp each salt and pepper. Finely grate zest of lemon into bowl and squeeze in 2 tsp juice; mix to combine. Fold in scallions and parsley. Spread onto middle of pastry.

4. Arrange tomatoes on tart, drizzle with oil and sprinkle with mint, sea salt and freshly ground pepper.

Dinner

Roasted Salmon

with Green Beans & Tomatoes

Simple yet so delicious, this omega-3–rich dinner is one to keep in your weekly rotation. Don't forget the Greek yogurt—it adds filling protein and a dash of creaminess.

PER SERVING
~330 cal,
15 g fat (3 g sat),
31 g pro,
445 mg sodium,
15 g carb, 5 g fiber

ACTIVE TIME 15 min.   **TOTAL TIME** 20 min.   **YIELDS** 4 servings

INGREDIENTS

- 1 pint grape tomatoes
- 1¼ lbs green beans, trimmed
- 3 anchovy fillets, chopped (optional)
- ½ cup pitted kalamata olives
- 6 cloves garlic, smashed
- 2 Tbsp olive oil, divided
- Kosher salt and pepper
- 1¼ lbs skinless salmon fillet, cut into 4 pieces
- Greek yogurt, for serving

DIRECTIONS

1. Heat oven to 425°F. On large rimmed baking sheet, toss tomatoes, beans, anchovies (if using), olives and garlic with 1 Tbsp oil and ¼ tsp pepper. Roast until vegetables are tender and beginning to brown, 12 to 15 min.

2. Meanwhile, heat remaining Tbsp oil in large skillet over medium heat. Season salmon with ¼ tsp each salt and pepper and cook until golden brown and opaque throughout, 4 to 5 min. per side. Serve with vegetables and yogurt if desired.

Dinner

White Bean Cassoulet
with Pork & Lentils

Let this hearty casserole simmer all day and your home will be brimming with its delicious scent.

PER SERVING
~465 cal, 13 g fat (4 g sat), 46 g pro, 775 mg sodium, 44 g carb, 13 g fiber

ACTIVE TIME 20 min. **TOTAL TIME** 6 hr. 25 min. (High) or 7 hr. 25 min. (Low) **YIELDS** 4 servings

INGREDIENTS

- 4 oz thick-cut bacon
- 2 cups low-sodium chicken broth
- ½ cup dry white wine
- 3 Tbsp tomato paste
- 8 cloves garlic, peeled and smashed
- 1 medium onion, chopped
- 1 14.5-oz can petite diced tomatoes, drained
- 2 lbs lean pork butt, trimmed and cut into 2-in. pieces (about 1¼ lbs total)
- 4 sprigs fresh thyme
- ½ cup dried brown lentils
- 1 15-oz can small white beans, rinsed

DIRECTIONS

1. Place bacon on paper-towel-lined plate and microwave on High until crisp, about 4 min. Cut into 1-in. pieces.

2. In 5- to 6-qt slow cooker, whisk together chicken broth, white wine and tomato paste. Add garlic, onion and tomatoes and mix to combine. Fold in pork, bacon and thyme.

3. Cook, covered, until pork easily pulls apart, 5 to 6 hr. on High or 7 to 8 hr. on Low.

4. Thirty-five min. before serving, discard thyme, then gently stir in lentils. With slow cooker on High, cover and continue cooking until lentils are just tender, 30 to 35 min. Gently fold in beans and cook until heated through, about 3 min. Serve with crusty bread if desired.

Dinner

Grilled Pork
with Charred Harissa Broccoli

Lean pork tenderloin gets a spicy pop of heat with peppery charred harissa broccoli.

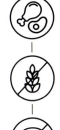

PER SERVING
~330 cal,
16.5 g fat (3.5 g sat),
38 g pro,
385 mg sodium,
8 g carb, 3 g fiber

ACTIVE TIME 10 min.   **TOTAL TIME** 30 min.   **YIELDS** 4 servings

INGREDIENTS

- 2 lemons
- 1½ lbs pork tenderloin
- 3 Tbsp plus 1 tsp olive oil
- Kosher salt and pepper
- 1 large head broccoli (about 1¼ lbs), trimmed and cut into large florets
- 2 Tbsp harissa

DIRECTIONS

1. Heat grill to medium-high. Finely grate zest of 1 lemon and set aside, then cut both lemons in half. Brush pork with 1 tsp oil and season with ½ tsp salt. Grill pork, turning occasionally, until an instant-read thermometer inserted into the center registers 140°F, 18 to 20 min. Transfer to cutting board and let rest at least 5 min.

2. Meanwhile, coat broccoli with 1 Tbsp olive oil and grill along with pork, until just tender and charred, 2 to 3 min. per side. Grill lemon until charred, 1 to 2 min.

3. Mix harissa with remaining 2 Tbsp oil and toss with broccoli; sprinkle with lemon zest.

4. Squeeze lemon halves over pork, then slice pork. Serve with broccoli and grilled lemon wedges.

Dinner

Vegetable Ramen
with Mushroom & Bok Choy

A classic favorite for all ages, this soup is packed with a variety of veggies. Slurping is encouraged!

PER SERVING
~300 cal, 10 g fat (4.5 g sat), 13 g pro, 1,075 mg sodium, 38 g carb, 4 g fiber

ACTIVE TIME 10 min.   **TOTAL TIME** 25 min.   **YIELDS** 4 servings

INGREDIENTS

- 3 scallions
- 1 3-oz piece ginger, peeled and very thinly sliced
- 5 Tbsp low-sodium tamari or soy sauce
- 6 oz ramen noodles
- 6 oz shiitake mushroom caps, thinly sliced
- 2 heads baby bok choy, stems thinly sliced and leaves halved lengthwise
- 4 oz snow peas, thinly sliced lengthwise
- 1 Tbsp rice vinegar
- 2 soft-medium boiled eggs, peeled and halved
- ½ cup cilantro sprigs
- Thinly sliced red chile, to taste

DIRECTIONS

1. Slice white parts of scallions and place in large pot with ginger and 8 cups water; bring to boil.

2. Stir in tamari, then add noodles and cook per pkg. directions, adding mushrooms and bok choy 3 min. after adding noodles. Remove from heat and stir in snow peas and vinegar.

3. Divide soup among 4 bowls and place 1 egg half on top of each. Slice remaining scallion greens and serve over soup along with cilantro and red chile.

Dinner

Shrimp Boil
with Sausage & Spinach

This dairy-free, protein-rich meal is a great option for a quick dinner. Once you try this blend of coriander, garlic, mustard and cayenne, you'll want to use it for everything.

PER SERVING
~345 cal, 13 g fat (3 g sat), 21 g pro, 1,125 mg sodium, 35 g carb, 4 g fiber

ACTIVE TIME 15 min.   **TOTAL TIME** 20 min.   **YIELDS** 4 servings

INGREDIENTS

- 1 lb small red-skinned new potatoes (about 12)
- 2 Tbsp olive oil
- 1 large onion, chopped
- Kosher salt and pepper
- 4 oz kielbasa, sliced
- 2 cloves garlic, finely chopped
- 1 tsp ground coriander
- ½ tsp ground mustard
- ¼ tsp cayenne
- ¾ lb large peeled and deveined shrimp (about 16)
- 1 cup corn kernels (from 1 ear, or thawed if frozen)
- 1 bunch spinach (about 12 oz), thick stems discarded, leaves roughly chopped

DIRECTIONS

1. Place potatoes on plate and microwave on High 2 min. Turn and microwave until just tender, 1 to 2 min. more. Cut in half.

2. Meanwhile, heat oil in large nonstick skillet on medium. Add onion and ½ tsp each salt and pepper and cook, stirring occasionally, until onion is tender, 4 to 6 min. Add potatoes and cook, stirring occasionally, until light golden brown, 2 to 3 min. Push to one side of pan.

3. Add kielbasa to other side of pan and cook, stirring occasionally, until starting to brown, 3 to 4 min. Add garlic, coriander, mustard and cayenne and cook, tossing, 1 min.

4. Add shrimp, corn and spinach; cover and cook, shaking pan occasionally, until shrimp are opaque throughout, 2 to 3 min.

Dinner

Wild Mushroom Toasts

PER SERVING
~475 cal,
16.5 g fat (6 g sat),
20 g pro,
800 mg sodium,
63 g carb, 6 g fiber

A secret superfood, wild mushrooms bring a warm and nutty taste to this savory dish. Paired with a touch of heat from red chiles, it's an exciting twist on everyday toast.

ACTIVE TIME 25 min.   **TOTAL TIME** 25 min.   **YIELDS** 4 servings

INGREDIENTS

- 2 Tbsp olive oil
- 1 lb mixed mushrooms, sliced or quartered if large
- Kosher salt and pepper
- 1 red chile, thinly sliced
- ¼ cup flat leaf parsley, chopped
- ½ cup fresh ricotta cheese
- ½ cup goat cheese, softened
- 4 thick slices country bread, toasted

DIRECTIONS

1. Heat large skillet on medium-high. Add oil and, in 3 batches, cook mushrooms, tossing occasionally, until golden brown and tender, 4 to 6 min. Season with salt and pepper, transfer to bowl and repeat with remaining mushrooms, adding more oil as necessary.

2. Add red chile to skillet and sauté until tender, 1 min.; mix with mushrooms and add parsley.

3. In bowl, combine ricotta and goat cheese. Spread evenly over toasts, then top with mushroom mixture.

TIP

You can prep and freeze this dish up to 2 months in advance. Line baking sheet with plastic. Prepare enchiladas, placing on top of plastic, but do not bake. Freeze until firm. Pop out of dish, wrap in plastic, and freeze. When ready to serve, unwrap and pop back into baking dish and let thaw overnight. Bake, covered, at 425°F for 20 min., then uncover and continue cooking as directed.

Dinner

Enchiladas Verdes

This popular gluten-free Mexican dish is served with a tangy salsa verde sauce. We cut down on cooking time by using rotisserie chicken, so you can have dinner on the table in about 30 minutes.

PER SERVING
~500 cal,
32 g fat (11 g sat),
30 g pro,
1,215 mg sodium,
39 g carb, 6 g fiber

ACTIVE TIME 25 min. **TOTAL TIME** 35 min. **YIELDS** 4 servings

INGREDIENTS

- ½ lb tomatillos (about 4), halved
- 2 cloves garlic (in their skins)
- 1 large onion, cut into 1-in.-thick wedges
- 1 large poblano pepper, halved, seeds discarded
- 1 jalapeño, halved, seeds discarded
- 1 Tbsp olive oil
- Kosher salt and pepper
- 7 Tbsp lime juice, divided
- 4 cups fresh cilantro, divided
- 8 corn tortillas
- 3 cups shredded rotisserie chicken
- 2 scallions, thinly sliced
- 6 oz Monterey Jack cheese, coarsely grated
- 1 small red onion, thinly sliced

DIRECTIONS

1. Make salsa verde: Heat broiler. On large rimmed baking sheet toss tomatillos, garlic, onion, poblano and jalapeño with oil and ½ tsp each salt and pepper. Broil, rotating pan every 5 min. until the vegetables are tender and charred, 15 min. total. Reduce temp to 425°F.

2. Discard skins from poblano and garlic and transfer all vegetables to blender. Add 3 Tbsp lime juice, 3 cups cilantro and ½ tsp salt and puree until smooth.

3. Make enchiladas: In bowl, toss chicken with scallions and 2 Tbsp lime juice. Fold in ½ cup cilantro and 1 cup cheese.

4. Spread ½ cup salsa in a 9- by 13-in. baking dish and transfer rest to bowl. Working with one tortilla at a time, dip in salsa then fill with about ½ cup chicken mixture. Roll chicken mixture in the tortillas and place seam-side down in the dish. Repeat.

5. Top with the remaining salsa and sprinkle with cheese. Bake until beginning to brown, 8 to 10 min.

6. Meanwhile, in small bowl, toss the red onion, remaining 2 Tbsp lime juice and pinch each salt and pepper. Serve over enchiladas and top with cilantro, if desired.

CHAPTER THREE: DINNER

Dinner

Fiery Black Bean Soup

A great dish for prepping ahead or batch cooking, this everyday soup gets its heat from fire-roasted tomatoes, peppers and spices.

PER SERVING
~325 cal,
6 g fat (1 g sat),
20 g pro,
705 mg sodium,
53 g carb, 18 g fiber

ACTIVE TIME 25 min.   **TOTAL TIME** 45 min.   **YIELDS** 4 servings

INGREDIENTS

- ½ lb tomatillos (about 4), halved
- 2 cloves unpeeled garlic
- 1 large onion, cut into 1-in.-thick wedges
- 1 large poblano pepper, halved and seeded
- 1 jalapeño, halved and seeded
- 1 Tbsp olive oil
- Kosher salt and pepper
- ½ tsp ground cumin
- ½ tsp ground coriander
- 4 cups low-sodium chicken broth
- 2 15-oz cans low-sodium black beans, rinsed
- 1 14.5-oz can fire-roasted diced tomatoes, drained
- 1 small red onion, thinly sliced
- 2 Tbsp fresh lime juice
- Cilantro leaves, for serving

DIRECTIONS

1. Heat broiler. On large rimmed baking sheet, toss tomatillos, garlic, onion, poblano and jalapeño with oil and ½ tsp each salt and pepper. Turn peppers cut sides down and broil, rotating pan every 5 min. until vegetables are tender and charred, 15 min. total.

2. Discard skins from poblanos and garlic. Finely chop vegetables and transfer to Dutch oven. Add cumin and coriander and cook on medium, stirring occasionally, 2 min. Add broth, beans and tomatoes and bring to a simmer; cook 4 min.

3. Meanwhile, make pickled onion: toss red onion with lime juice and pinch each salt and pepper; let sit at least 10 min. Serve soup topped with pickled onion and cilantro.

TIP

Double soup and freeze half in pint- or quart-sized containers for up to 2 months. Thaw in refrigerator overnight then warm in saucepan over medium heat until heated through. Prepare pickled onions just before serving.

Dinner

Creamy Corn Chowder

Corn and potatoes make this vegetarian soup extra creamy and comforting. A pinch of caraway seeds brings a slightly earthy flavor to each spoonful.

PER SERVING
~425 cal,
15 g fat (5 g sat),
14 g pro,
510 mg sodium,
66 g carb, 6 g fiber

ACTIVE TIME 25 min.   **TOTAL TIME** 45 min.   **YIELDS** 4 servings

INGREDIENTS

- 3½ lbs golden new potatoes, halved (quartered if large)
- 4 small onions, cut into ¼-in.-thick wedges
- 4 Tbsp olive oil
- 12 sprigs fresh thyme
- Kosher salt and pepper
- 1 tsp caraway seeds
- 4 cups low-sodium chicken broth
- 1 lb frozen corn, thawed
- ¼ cup heavy cream
- 2 Tbsp fresh lemon juice
- Crumbled bacon and thinly sliced scallions, for topping, if desired

DIRECTIONS

1. Heat oven to 450°F. Prepare vegetables: On large rimmed baking sheet, toss potatoes and onions with oil, thyme and ¾ tsp each salt and pepper. Transfer half to second sheet and toss with caraway seeds. Arrange all potatoes cut side down and roast both sheets, rotating positions of sheets halfway through, until golden brown and tender, 25 to 30 min. Set aside vegetables without caraway seeds.

2. Discard thyme from the vegetables and transfer half of them to large pot. Add chicken broth and bring to boil. Using immersion blender (or standard blender), puree until smooth.

3. Add corn and remaining roasted vegetables to pot and bring to simmer. Stir in heavy cream, fresh lemon juice and ½ tsp each salt and pepper. Serve topped with crumbled bacon and thinly sliced scallions, if desired.

Dinner

Charred Shrimp & Avocado Salad

Grilled shrimp and creamy avocado partner perfectly with tropical fruit in this easy salad.

PER SERVING
~420 cal,
23.5 g fat (3.5 g sat),
35 g pro,
1,595 mg sodium,
20 g carb, 4 g fiber

ACTIVE TIME 10 min. **TOTAL TIME** 25 min. **YIELDS** 4 servings

INGREDIENTS

- 2 Tbsp fresh lemon juice
- 4 Tbsp olive oil, divided
- Kosher salt and pepper
- ½ small red onion, thinly sliced
- ½ small pineapple, peeled, trimmed and cut into ½-in.-thick slices
- 2½ lbs large peeled and deveined shrimp
- ½ English cucumber, sliced into half-moons
- ½ bunch upland watercress
- 1 avocado, quartered

DIRECTIONS

1. In large bowl, whisk together lemon juice, 2 Tbsp oil and ¼ tsp each salt and pepper. Toss with onion.

2. Heat grill, grill-pan or broiler. Brush pineapple with 1 Tbsp oil and toss shrimp with remaining Tbsp oil. Broil until pineapple is slightly charred and shrimp is opaque throughout, 5 to 8 min.

3. Cut pineapple into smaller pieces and add to bowl with onion along with cucumber and shrimp and toss to combine. Fold in watercress and serve with avocado.

Dinner

Shrimp Rolls

Bookmark this recipe for the next time you have leftover shrimp. Combined with crunchy sliced veggies and gochujang—a sweet and spicy sauce—it makes for a quick and easy Asian-inspired sandwich.

PER SERVING
~375 cal, 14.5 g fat (2.5 g sat), 40 g pro, 1,525 mg sodium, 30 g carb, 2 g fiber

ACTIVE TIME 15 min.   **TOTAL TIME** 15 min.   **YIELDS** 4 servings

INGREDIENTS

- 1 medium carrot, peeled into ribbons
- 2 scallions, cut into 2-in. pieces then thinly sliced lengthwise
- 4 small radishes, thinly sliced
- 4 Tbsp lime juice, divided
- 3 Tbsp mayo
- 1 Tbsp gochujang
- 1½ lbs broiled or grilled shrimp, halved or cut into thirds, if large
- ¼ cup small mint leaves
- 4 split-top hot dog rolls, toasted

DIRECTIONS

1. In medium bowl, toss carrot, scallions and radishes with 2 Tbsp lime juice.
2. In large bowl, whisk together mayo, gochujang and 2 Tbsp lime juice. Add shrimp and toss to coat; fold in mint.
3. Fill buns with shrimp mixture and top with carrot ribbon salad.

TIP
Top this dish with a fried egg for an extra dose of creaminess and protein. Per 1 egg and 2 tsp butter: 139 cal, 12.5 g fat (6.5 g sat), 6 g pro, 132 mg sodium, 0 g carb, 0 g fiber

Dinner

Wild Mushroom Risotto

You might not think "risotto" and "low-calorie" are compatible, but this version is high in filling fiber and delivers a protein boost from the fried eggs.

PER SERVING
~450 cal, 16.5 g fat (3.5 g sat), 16 g pro, 470 mg sodium, 64 g carb, 5 g fiber

ACTIVE TIME 30 min.   **TOTAL TIME** 40 min.   **YIELDS** 4 servings

INGREDIENTS

- 4 Tbsp olive oil, divided
- 1 large onion, finely chopped
- 4 cloves garlic, pressed, divided
- 2 cups Arborio rice
- 1 cup dry white wine
- 4 cups low-sodium chicken broth or water
- Kosher salt and pepper
- 1 cup finely grated Parmesan cheese
- 1 lb mixed wild mushrooms, stemmed and sliced
- 1 red chile, thinly sliced
- 2 sprigs thyme, broken into small pieces
- Fried eggs, for serving

DIRECTIONS

1. Heat 2 Tbsp oil in large saucepan on medium. Add onion and cook, covered, stirring occasionally, until tender, 6 to 8 min. Stir in half of garlic and cook 2 min. Add rice and wine and cook, stirring, until wine is absorbed, about 3 min.

2. Add broth (or water) and ¾ tsp each salt and pepper and bring to a boil. Reduce heat and simmer, covered, until liquid is absorbed and rice is tender, 18 to 20 min. Stir in Parmesan. Spread 3 cups risotto on parchment-lined baking sheet and let cool.

3. Meanwhile, heat remaining 2 Tbsp oil in large skillet on medium-high. Cook half of mushrooms, tossing occasionally, until golden brown, 6 to 8 min.; transfer to plate. Repeat with remaining mushrooms; when they are browned, add chile, thyme and remaining garlic and cook 2 min. more. Toss with first batch of mushrooms to distribute flavorings.

4. Serve mushrooms over risotto, topped with fried egg if desired.

Dinner

Coconut Curry Chicken

PER SERVING
~485 cal,
28 g fat (9.5 g sat),
41 g pro,
645 mg sodium,
21 g carb, 4 g fiber

Cashew butter is the genius, secret pantry ingredient in this delicious dinner. It adds body and richness that contrasts nicely with all those flavorful spices.

ACTIVE TIME 25 min.   **TOTAL TIME** 40 min.   **YIELDS** 6 servings

INGREDIENTS

- 3 Tbsp olive oil, divided
- 2 lbs boneless, skinless chicken breasts, cut into 1-in. chunks
- Kosher salt and pepper
- 1 large onion, chopped
- 4 cloves garlic, pressed
- 1 red chile, finely chopped
- 1 2-in. piece fresh ginger, peeled and coarsely grated
- 1 Tbsp garam masala
- 1 28-oz can crushed tomatoes
- ¾ cup unsweetened coconut milk
- ½ cup cashew butter *OR Sunflower*
- Rice, cilantro, chopped cashews and sliced red chiles, for serving

top w/ cashews Roasted

DIRECTIONS

1. Heat 2 Tbsp oil in large Dutch oven on medium. Season chicken with ½ tsp each salt and pepper and cook, tossing often, until no longer pink, 5 min.; transfer to bowl.

2. Reduce heat to medium-low; add remaining Tbsp oil to pot, then onion, and cook, covered, stirring occasionally, until tender and beginning to brown, 6 to 8 min. Stir in garlic and chile and cook 1 min. Stir in ginger, garam masala and ½ tsp salt and cook 1 min.

3. Add tomatoes, coconut milk and cashew butter and mix to combine. Return chicken and any juices to pot and gently simmer, covered, stirring occasionally, until chicken is cooked through, 6 to 8 min. Serve over rice, topped with cilantro, cashews and chiles if desired.

Delishious!!
w/ Aunt Wendy
July 2022

Dinner

Mini Meatballs
with Garlicky Tomatoes

A crowd-pleasing appetizer, these low-carb mini meatballs can be prepared ahead of time and reheated before serving.

PER SERVING
~310 cal,
16.5 g fat (5.5 g sat),
29 g pro,
505 mg sodium,
11 g carb, 2 g fiber

ACTIVE TIME 45 min.   **TOTAL TIME** 45 min.   **YIELDS** 4 servings

INGREDIENTS

- 1   3-in. piece baguette (about 1 oz)
- 2   large eggs
- 4   cloves garlic (2 finely chopped, 2 crushed with press)
- 2   cups packed baby spinach (1 cup finely chopped, 1 cup finely sliced)
- ¼   cup Parmesan cheese, finely grated
- ½   tsp dried oregano
-     Kosher salt and pepper
- 1   lb ground beef
- 1   lb Campari tomatoes
- 1   Tbsp olive oil

DIRECTIONS

1. Heat broiler and line large rimmed baking sheet with nonstick foil. Tear baguette into pieces and soak in ¼ cup water until absorbed, then squeeze out all moisture and transfer to large bowl. Add eggs, chopped garlic, chopped spinach, Parmesan, oregano and ½ tsp each salt and pepper and mix to combine. Add beef and mix until combined. Form into tiny balls (about 1 level tsp each, about 92 balls) and place on prepared baking sheet. Broil until browned, 6 to 8 min.

2. Halve tomatoes and arrange, cut sides up, on second baking sheet. Drizzle with oil and sprinkle tops with pressed garlic and pinch each salt and pepper. Broil until garlic is fragrant, 3 to 4 min. Serve meatballs with tomatoes and sliced spinach.

Dinner

Oil & Vinegar Chicken Cutlet Sandwiches

PER SERVING
~330 cal, 7 g fat (1 g sat), 33 g pro, 705 mg sodium, 32 g carb, 3 g fiber

There are few low-calorie condiment combos as deliciously simple as oil and vinegar. Be sure to use a crusty baguette to soak up all the flavor!

ACTIVE TIME 20 min. **TOTAL TIME** 20 min. **YIELDS** 4 servings

INGREDIENTS

- ½ small red onion, thinly sliced
- 1 Tbsp red wine vinegar
- Kosher salt and pepper
- 1 lb boneless, skinless chicken breasts
- 1 Tbsp olive oil
- 6 cups baby spinach
- 4 5-in. pieces baguette, split and toasted

DIRECTIONS

1. In a small bowl, toss onion with vinegar and ⅛ tsp each salt and pepper; set aside.

2. Cut chicken into 6 thin cutlets. Heat oil in large skillet on medium-high. Season chicken with ½ tsp each salt and pepper and cook until browned and cooked through, 2 min. per side; transfer to cutting board.

3. Add spinach to skillet, season with salt and pepper and cook until just beginning to wilt.

4. Slice chicken and sandwich between baguette halves with spinach and onions.

Dinner

Pan-Fried Chicken

with Lemony Roasted Broccoli

You don't need much more than a handful of pantry staples to create this simple and delicious main.

PER SERVING
~365 cal,
15.5 g fat (2.5 g sat),
44 g pro,
375 mg sodium,
15 g carb, 5 g fiber

ACTIVE TIME 25 min. **TOTAL TIME** 35 min. **YIELDS** 4 servings

---

INGREDIENTS

- 1½ lbs broccoli, cut into florets
- 2 cloves garlic, thinly sliced
- 3 Tbsp olive oil, divided
- Kosher salt and pepper
- 4 6-oz boneless, skinless chicken breasts
- 1 cup all-purpose flour
- 1 lemon, cut into ½-in. pieces
- 2 Tbsp lemon juice

DIRECTIONS

1. Heat oven to 425°F. On rimmed baking sheet, toss broccoli and garlic with 1 Tbsp oil and ¼ tsp each salt and pepper; roast 10 min.

2. Meanwhile, pound chicken breasts to even thickness, season with ¼ tsp each salt and pepper, then coat in flour. Heat 1 Tbsp oil in large skillet on medium-high and cook chicken until golden brown, 3 to 5 min. per side. Nestle chicken amidst broccoli and roast until chicken is cooked through and broccoli is golden brown and tender, about 6 min.

3. Return skillet to medium heat; add remaining Tbsp oil, then lemon pieces, and cook, stirring, until beginning to brown, 3 min. Add lemon juice and ⅓ cup water and cook, stirring and scraping up any browned bits, for 1 min. Spoon over chicken and serve with broccoli.

TIP

To save a little time, you can prep broccoli and lemons and store for up to 2 days before cooking.

CHAPTER THREE: DINNER

Dinner

Cheesy Chicken & Broccoli Casserole

PER SERVING
~375 cal,
14 g fat (4.5 g sat),
37 g pro,
800 mg sodium,
25 g carb, 3 g fiber

Craving comfort food? This dish has all the piping hot, creamy goodness of a classic casserole but with less than 400 calories per serving.

ACTIVE TIME 20 min. **TOTAL TIME** 40 min. **YIELDS** 4 servings

INGREDIENTS

- 1 lb boneless, skinless chicken breasts
- Kosher salt and pepper
- 1 Tbsp plus 1 tsp olive oil
- 1 yellow onion, finely chopped
- 1 clove garlic, pressed
- 3 Tbsp all-purpose flour
- 3 oz Parmesan cheese, finely grated
- 12 oz broccoli florets
- 3 oz roughly torn baguette (about 2 cups)

DIRECTIONS

1. Heat oven to 425°F. Cut chicken into 1½-in. pieces; season with ½ tsp each salt and pepper. Heat 1 Tbsp oil in large skillet on medium-high and cook chicken until browned on 1 side, about 2 min.; transfer to plate. Reduce heat to medium-low, then add onion; sauté until tender, 5 min. Stir in garlic; cook 1 min.

2. Sprinkle flour over onion and cook, stirring, 1 min. Slowly stir in 1½ cups water, scraping up any browned bits, then Parmesan. In 2½-qt shallow baking dish, toss together chicken and broccoli. Spoon onion mixture over top and bake 10 min.

3. Meanwhile, in food processor, pulse baguette with remaining tsp oil to form coarse crumbs; sprinkle over casserole and bake until golden brown, about 15 min.

Dinner

Classic Omelet & Greens

Breakfast for dinner or dinner for breakfast? Either way this classic omelet won't disappoint. Pair it with a simple green salad for a satisfying meal.

PER SERVING
~330 cal, 27.5 g fat (9.5 g sat), 16 g pro, 575 mg sodium, 6 g carb, 1 g fiber

ACTIVE TIME 20 min. **TOTAL TIME** 20 min. **YIELDS** 4 servings

INGREDIENTS

- 3 Tbsp olive oil, divided
- 1 yellow onion, finely chopped
- 8 large eggs
- Kosher salt
- 2 Tbsp unsalted butter
- 1 oz Parmesan cheese, finely grated
- 2 Tbsp fresh lemon juice
- 3 oz baby spinach

DIRECTIONS

1. Heat 1 Tbsp oil in large nonstick skillet on medium. Add onion and sauté until tender, about 6 min. Transfer to small bowl.

2. In large bowl, whisk together eggs, 1 Tbsp water and ½ tsp salt. Return skillet to medium and add butter. Add eggs and cook, stirring constantly with rubber spatula, until eggs are partially set. Turn heat to low and cover pan tightly, cooking until eggs are just set, 4 to 5 min. Top with Parmesan and cooked onion; fold in half.

3. In a medium bowl, whisk together lemon juice and remaining 2 Tbsp olive oil. Toss spinach with vinaigrette and serve with omelet.

Dinner

Beef Kofte
with Kale & Chickpea Salad

High in protein and rich in fiber, spiced beef, chickpeas and greens come together in this Middle Eastern–inspired dish.

PER SERVING
~385 cal, 20 g fat (5 g sat), 29 g pro, 470 mg sodium, 23 g carb, 7 g fiber

ACTIVE TIME 20 min. **TOTAL TIME** 20 min. **YIELDS** 4 servings

INGREDIENTS

- 1 lemon
- 1 lb ground beef
- 2 cloves garlic, finely chopped
- 1½ tsp ground cumin
- 1½ tsp ground coriander
- Kosher salt and pepper
- 3 Tbsp olive oil, divided
- ½ tsp dried oregano
- 1 small red onion, thinly sliced
- 1 15-oz can chickpeas, rinsed
- 4 cups baby kale
- 1 pint cherry tomatoes, halved

DIRECTIONS

1. Finely grate zest of lemon and squeeze 3 Tbsp juice into small bowl. In large bowl, combine beef, garlic, cumin, coriander, lemon zest, 1 Tbsp lemon juice and ½ tsp each salt and pepper. Form 12 flat, ovular cakes (these are the kofte).

2. Heat 1 Tbsp oil in large skillet and cook kofte until browned, 90 seconds per side. In another large bowl, whisk oregano with remaining 2 Tbsp oil and remaining 2 Tbsp lemon juice. Add onion and chickpeas and toss to combine. Let sit 5 min., then toss with kale and tomatoes. Serve with kofte.

CHAPTER THREE: DINNER

Dinner

Hearty Bean & Beef Chili

PER SERVING
~375 cal,
17 g fat (4.5 g sat),
30 g pro,
480 mg sodium,
25 g carb, 11 g fiber

The essential low-calorie chili, this dish has it all: minimal cleanup, warming spices and plenty of protein. Swap the beef for ground turkey or chicken to lighten it up even more.

ACTIVE TIME 30 min.   **TOTAL TIME** 40 min.   **YIELDS** 4 servings

INGREDIENTS

- 2 Tbsp olive oil, divided
- 1 lb ground beef
- 2 tsp ground cumin
- 2 tsp chili powder
- Kosher salt and pepper
- 1 yellow onion, finely chopped
- 1 clove garlic, pressed
- 1 lb tomatoes, finely chopped *[or canned]*
- 1 15-oz can cannellini beans, rinsed

DIRECTIONS

1. Heat 1 Tbsp oil in large pot on medium. Add beef, cumin, chili powder and ½ tsp each salt and pepper and cook, breaking up beef, until browned, about 10 min. Transfer beef to paper-towel-lined plate.

2. Return pot to medium; add remaining Tbsp olive oil, then onion, and cook until tender, 4 to 5 min. Stir in garlic and cook 1 min. Add tomatoes and cook until they release their juices, about 5 min. Add 2 cups water and simmer until slightly thickened, about 10 min.

3. Transfer half of beans to small bowl and mash with fork. Add to pot along with whole beans and reserved beef and heat through.

Dinner

Paprika Chicken

with **Crispy Chickpeas & Tomatoes**

Don't skimp on the paprika: this versatile spice infuses a sweet red pepper flavor and a bold red hue to whatever it touches. It's the key ingredient to this comforting chicken dinner.

PER SERVING
~390 cal,
16 g fat (2.5 g sat),
40 g pro,
590 mg sodium,
21 g carb, 6 g fiber

ACTIVE TIME 15 min.   **TOTAL TIME** 20 min.   **YIELDS** 4 servings

INGREDIENTS

- 12 oz tomatoes
- 8 cloves garlic, smashed, in their skins
- 1 15-oz can chickpeas, rinsed
- 3 Tbsp olive oil, divided
  Kosher salt and pepper
- 4 6-oz boneless, skinless chicken breasts
- 2 tsp paprika

DIRECTIONS

1. Heat oven to 425°F. On rimmed baking sheet, toss tomatoes, garlic and chickpeas with 2 Tbsp oil and ¼ tsp each salt and pepper. Roast 10 min.

2. Heat remaining Tbsp oil in large skillet on medium. Season chicken with paprika and ½ tsp each salt and pepper and cook until golden brown on one side, 5 to 6 min. Flip and cook 1 min. more.

3. Transfer to baking sheet with tomatoes and chickpeas and roast until cooked through, 6 min. more. Before serving, discard garlic skins.

Dinner

Grilled Chicken Skewers & Kale Caesar

Serve these simple grilled chicken skewers with a creamy, garlicky kale Caesar salad for a light summer meal that can be on the table fast.

PER SERVING
~465 cal,
25 g fat (5 g sat),
41 g pro,
705 mg sodium,
18 g carb, 2 g fiber

ACTIVE TIME 35 min. **TOTAL TIME** 45 min. **YIELDS** 4 servings

INGREDIENTS

- 2 lemons
- 1 lbs boneless, skinless chicken breasts
- Kosher salt and pepper
- 8 thick slices baguette
- 1 clove garlic, halved, plus ½ small clove garlic, finely grated
- 1 large egg yolk
- ½ tsp Dijon mustard
- ⅓ cup olive oil
- ¼ cup grated Parmesan cheese
- 5 oz baby kale

DIRECTIONS

1. Cut 1 lemon in half. From remaining lemon, finely grate 1 tsp zest and squeeze 4 Tbsp juice.

2. Cut chicken into 1½-in. chunks; thread onto skewers and season with ¼ tsp each salt and pepper. Grill until cooked through, 3 to 4 min. per side. Grill 1 lemon half, cut side down, until charred, 1 to 2 min.; squeeze over chicken. Grill bread until toasted, rub both sides with garlic halves, then cut into cubes.

3. In large bowl, whisk together lemon zest and juice, egg yolk, mustard, grated garlic and ½ tsp salt. Slowly whisk in oil. Fold in Parmesan, then kale and croutons, and season with pepper. Serve with chicken.

Dinner

Chicken & Broccoli Parchment Packets

Quick and easy with minimal clean-up time, this recipe uses parchment paper to steam chicken and broccoli to perfection. Top it off with lemon zest and vinaigrette for an additional layer of flavor.

PER SERVING
~330 cal, 12 g fat (2 g sat), 43 g pro, 485 mg sodium, 14 g carb, 5 g fiber

ACTIVE TIME 35 min.   **TOTAL TIME** 45 min.   **YIELDS** 4 servings

INGREDIENTS

- 1¼ lbs broccoli, stems sliced, crowns cut into small florets
- 2 cloves garlic, pressed
- 2 Tbsp olive oil, divided
- Kosher salt and pepper
- 4 6-oz boneless, skinless chicken breasts
- 1 lemon
- ½ small red onion, finely chopped
- 8 oz tomatoes, chopped

DIRECTIONS

1. Heat oven to 400°F. Toss broccoli with garlic, 1 Tbsp oil and ¼ tsp each salt and pepper. Divide among four 12-in. squares of parchment. Season chicken with ¼ tsp each salt and pepper and place on top of broccoli. Cover with second piece of parchment and fold up edges to seal. Place packets on 2 rimmed baking sheets and roast 15 min.

2. Meanwhile, finely grate zest of lemon and squeeze 2 Tbsp juice. In medium bowl, combine onion, lemon juice, remaining Tbsp oil and ¼ tsp each salt and pepper. Let sit 4 min., then toss with tomatoes. Cut open packets; top with vinaigrette and lemon zest.

Dinner

Striped Bass
with Radish Salsa Verde

Rich in flavor and nutrients, this dish can be made ahead for busy weeknights. Even better, you can use any leftover radish greens in salsas, sauces and sautés.

PER SERVING
~465 cal, 35.5 g fat (5 g sat), 33 g pro, 640 mg sodium, 3 g carb, 1 g fiber

ACTIVE TIME 35 min. **TOTAL TIME** 40 min. **YIELDS** 4 servings

INGREDIENTS

- 1 clove garlic, pressed
- 1 Tbsp anchovy paste or 3 anchovy fillets, finely chopped
- ½ small red onion, finely chopped
- 1 Tbsp red wine vinegar
- ½ cup plus 1 Tbsp olive oil, divided
- 1 bunch radishes, diced, leaves separated and finely chopped
- 1 cup flat-leaf parsley leaves, finely chopped
- 1 tsp tarragon leaves, finely chopped
- 4 6-oz fillets striped bass, patted dry
- Kosher salt and pepper

DIRECTIONS

1. In medium bowl, combine garlic, anchovy paste, onion and vinegar and let sit for 5 min.

2. Stir in ½ cup oil, then radishes and greens, parsley and tarragon.

3. In medium skillet, heat remaining Tbsp oil on medium. Season fish with ½ tsp each salt and pepper and cook, skin side down, until skin is crisp and golden brown, about 7 min. Flip and cook until fish is opaque throughout, 3 to 6 min. more. Serve topped with radish salsa verde.

Dinner

Spring Herb Frittata

Using a variety of fresh spring herbs, this light and colorful popular brunch dish is guaranteed to impress your guests.

PER SERVING
~305 cal, 26.5 g fat (8 g sat), 12 g pro, 375 mg sodium, 6 g carb, 2 g fiber

ACTIVE TIME 15 min.   **TOTAL TIME** 40 min.   **YIELDS** 4 servings

INGREDIENTS

- ¼ cup crème fraîche, at room temperature
- 2 Tbsp chopped chives
- 6 large eggs
- 6 scallions, cut into 1-in. pieces
- 2 cups flat-leaf parsley leaves, plus more for topping
- 2 cups cilantro leaves and tender stems, plus more for topping
- ½ cup dill fronds, plus more for topping
- 2 Tbsp tarragon leaves, plus more for topping
- 4 Tbsp olive oil, divided
- Kosher salt and pepper

DIRECTIONS

1. Heat oven to 350°F. In small bowl, stir together crème fraîche and chives; set aside.

2. In large bowl, lightly beat eggs. In food processor, pulse scallions, parsley, cilantro, dill, tarragon and 2 Tbsp oil until evenly and finely chopped. Add to bowl with eggs, along with ½ tsp each salt and pepper, and mix to combine.

3. Heat remaining 2 Tbsp oil in medium skillet on medium until shimmering, about 2 min. Add egg mixture and cook until edges have begun to sizzle and set, about 2 min. Transfer skillet to oven and bake until center is just set, 18 to 20 min. Let rest at least 5 min. Serve with chive crème fraîche. Sprinkle with more herbs, if desired.

Dinner

Fennel Pasta Pomodoro

PER SERVING
~455 cal,
9 g fat (1.5 g sat),
14 g pro,
665 mg sodium,
76 g carb, 6 g fiber

A modern version of an Italian classic, where fennel seeds and fresh rosemary star as the secret ingredients.

ACTIVE TIME 25 min.   **TOTAL TIME** 25 min.   **YIELDS** 4 servings

INGREDIENTS

- 12 oz spaghetti
- 2 Tbsp olive oil
- 1 onion, finely chopped
- Kosher salt and pepper
- 3 cloves garlic, finely chopped
- 1 Tbsp fresh rosemary, chopped
- 1 tsp fennel seeds, coarsely cracked
- 1 28-oz can whole peeled tomatoes

DIRECTIONS

1. Cook pasta per pkg. directions.

2. Heat oil in large skillet on medium. Add onion and ½ tsp each salt and pepper and sauté until tender, 5 to 6 min. Stir in garlic, rosemary and fennel seeds and cook 2 min.

3. Using kitchen shears, while tomatoes are still in can, cut them into smaller chunks and add to pan along with juices, then simmer until slightly thickened, 2 to 3 min. Toss with pasta.

Dinner

Savory Lentil Waffles

Who says waffles need to stick to breakfast? (Or that breakfast waffles need to be sweet?) These make a perfect base for a spiced lentil-arugula salad.

PER SERVING
~389 cal,
16 g fat (2 g sat),
13 g pro,
503 mg sodium,
50 g carb, 10 g fiber

ACTIVE TIME 20 min.   **TOTAL TIME** 20 min.   **YIELDS** 4 servings

INGREDIENTS

- 1 14.5-oz can lentils, rinsed
- ¼ small red onion, thinly sliced
- ¼ cup golden raisins, chopped
- 3 Tbsp olive oil
- 3 Tbsp sherry vinegar
- 1 cup store-bought waffle mix
- 1 tsp curry powder
- ¼ tsp ground coriander
- Kosher salt and pepper
- 4 cups baby arugula
- ¼ cup roasted almonds, chopped
- Plain Greek yogurt, for serving

DIRECTIONS

1. In medium bowl, combine lentils, red onion, raisins, olive oil and sherry vinegar. Set aside.

2. In large bowl, whisk together waffle mix, curry powder, ground coriander and ⅛ tsp each salt and pepper. Prepare and cook 2 waffles in waffle maker per manufacturer's directions.

3. When waffles are cooked, toss arugula and almonds with lentil mixture.

4. Cut waffles into pieces and spread with plain Greek yogurt if desired. Top with lentil salad.

Dinner

Soy-Glazed Meatloaf

When you don't have time to run to the store, make this timeless comfort food, which relies heavily on pantry staples. Bonus: it tastes even better the next day.

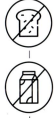

PER SERVING
~275 cal, 14.5 g fat (5.5 g sat), 23.5 g pro, 430 mg sodium, 11 g carb, 1 g fiber

ACTIVE TIME 20 min. **TOTAL TIME** 1 hr. 5 min. **YIELDS** 6 servings

INGREDIENTS

- 2 Tbsp ketchup
- 1 Tbsp brown sugar
- 1 Tbsp plus 1 tsp reduced-sodium soy sauce
- 2 large eggs
- 1 Tbsp balsamic vinegar
- Kosher salt and pepper
- ½ cup panko breadcrumbs
- 1 small onion, coarsely grated
- ½ cup fresh flat-leaf parsley, finely chopped
- 1½ lbs ground beef chuck
- Mixed green salad, for serving

DIRECTIONS

1. Heat oven to 375°F. Line large rimmed baking sheet with foil. In bowl, combine ketchup, brown sugar and 1 tsp soy sauce. Set aside.

2. In large bowl, whisk together eggs, balsamic vinegar, remaining Tbsp soy sauce and ½ tsp each salt and pepper; stir in breadcrumbs and let sit 2 min. Add onion and parsley and mix to combine.

3. Add beef and mix just until incorporated. Transfer mixture to prepared baking sheet and shape into 9- by 3½-in. loaf.

4. Brush loaf with ketchup mixture. Bake until internal temp registers 150°F, 40 to 45 min. Let rest 5 min. before slicing. Serve with salad if desired.

Dinner

Slow Cooker BBQ Jackfruit Sandwich
with Pineapple Slaw

This recipe proves that you don't need meat for a successful BBQ. Jackfruit adds a meaty texture with around 150 calories per cup, while pineapple adds a pop of flavor.

PER SERVING
~270 cal, 8 g fat (0.5 g sat), 8 g pro, 665 mg sodium, 50 g carb, 5 g fiber

ACTIVE TIME 25 min. **TOTAL TIME** 3 hr. 55 min. **YIELDS** 8 servings

INGREDIENTS

- 1 8-oz can tomato sauce
- 2 Tbsp packed brown sugar
- 2 Tbsp molasses
- 1 Tbsp chili powder
- Kosher salt and pepper
- 2 large cloves garlic, finely chopped
- 2 small red onions, finely chopped, divided
- 2 14-oz cans young, green jackfruit in brine or water (not syrup), rinsed
- 2 Tbsp fresh lime juice
- 1 tsp agave nectar
- ¼ small ripe pineapple, peeled, cored and cut into matchsticks
- 1 cup fresh cilantro leaves
- 12 small slider buns, split
- Sliced avocado

DIRECTIONS

1. In slow cooker, combine tomato sauce, sugar, molasses, chili powder, ¾ cup water and ½ tsp salt. Add garlic and 1¾ onions and stir into sauce along with jackfruit. Cover and cook on High until very tender, 3 to 4 hr.

2. Ten min. before serving, whisk together lime juice, agave nectar and ¼ tsp each salt and pepper. Toss remaining onion slices with lime juice mixture.

3. Using two forks, gently break up jackfruit. Toss onion with pineapple and fold in cilantro. Divide jackfruit among rolls and top with avocado and pineapple slaw.

Dinner

Speedy Eggplant Parmesan

This streamlined version of eggplant Parmesan reduces your time and effort in the kitchen but delivers big on flavor—and in under 45 minutes!

PER SERVING
~485 cal,
23 g fat (7 g sat),
23 g pro,
1,115 mg sodium,
70 g carb, 8 g fiber

ACTIVE TIME 20 min.   **TOTAL TIME** 40 min.   **YIELDS** 4 servings

---

INGREDIENTS

- ½ cup all-purpose flour
- 1 large egg plus 1 egg white
- 1 cup panko breadcrumbs
- ½ cup freshly grated Parmesan cheese
- ½ tsp garlic powder
- Kosher salt and pepper
- 1 Tbsp olive oil
- 1 small eggplant (about 12 oz), cut into long ½-in.-thick sticks
- 1 16- to 18-oz pkg. cheese ravioli
- 1 cup jarred marinara sauce, warmed
- Shredded fresh mozzarella, for serving

DIRECTIONS

1. Heat oven to 450°F. Line large baking sheet with nonstick foil.

2. Place flour on plate and beat egg and egg white in shallow bowl. In second shallow bowl or pie plate, combine breadcrumbs, Parmesan, garlic powder, ½ tsp salt and ¼ tsp pepper, then toss with olive oil.

3. Coat eggplant sticks in flour, then egg (letting any excess drip off), then coat in breadcrumb mixture, pressing gently to help it adhere. Transfer to prepared baking sheet and roast, turning halfway through, until golden brown, 15 to 18 min.

4. Meanwhile, cook ravioli according to pkg. directions. Drain, divide among plates and top with sauce. Cut eggplant sticks into pieces and scatter on top of ravioli. Serve with shredded fresh mozzarella, if desired.

CHAPTER THREE: DINNER

Meyer Lemon Madeleines
p. 273

Chapter Four

Dessert

Dessert

Mini Chocolate Chip Sandwiches

PER SERVING
~155 cal,
8.5 g fat (5 g sat),
2 g pro,
90 mg sodium,
19 g carb, 1 g fiber

They may be mini, but these cookie sandwiches, filled with rich chocolate frosting, pack a big punch of flavor.

ACTIVE TIME 25 min.   **TOTAL TIME** 35 min.   **YIELDS** 25 servings

INGREDIENTS

- 1½ cups cake flour
- ½ tsp baking powder
- ½ tsp baking soda
- ½ tsp kosher salt
- ½ cup unsalted butter (1 stick), at room temp
- ¼ cup plus 2 Tbsp granulated sugar
- 2 Tbsp brown sugar
- 1 large egg
- ½ tsp pure vanilla extract
- 4 oz bittersweet chocolate, roughly chopped
- 4 oz semisweet chocolate, roughly chopped
- Chocolate frosting, for sandwiching

DIRECTIONS

1. Line 2 large baking sheets with parchment paper. In medium bowl, sift together cake flour, baking powder, baking soda and salt. Set aside.

2. Using electric mixer on medium speed, beat butter and sugars until light and fluffy, 3 min. Reduce mixer speed to low and mix in egg, followed by vanilla.

3. Add flour mixture in 3 additions, mixing until just incorporated. Mix in chocolate.

4. Scoop rounded tsp of dough and arrange on prepared baking sheets 2 in. apart. Flatten tops slightly and freeze for 10 min.

5. Heat oven to 350°F. Bake, rotating pans after 5 min., until cookies are puffed and edges are beginning to turn golden brown, 7 to 8 min. total. Let cool completely, then sandwich together with chocolate frosting.

CHAPTER FOUR: DESSERT

Dessert

Eggnog Truffles

A glass of eggnog isn't quite low-calorie, so we transformed the creamy holiday beverage into bite-size sweets.

PER SERVING
~118 cal,
7 g fat (4.5 g sat),
1 g pro,
40 mg sodium,
12 g carb, 0 g fiber

ACTIVE TIME 45 min. **TOTAL TIME** 3 hr. 15 min. **YIELDS** 45 servings

INGREDIENTS

- ½ cup heavy cream
- 2 oz cream cheese, at room temperature
- 1 Tbsp dark rum
- 24 oz white chocolate, chopped, divided
- 2 cups (7 oz) gingersnap cookie crumbs, from about 44 cookies (we used Anna's Ginger Thins)
- Freshly grated nutmeg and cinnamon, for topping

DIRECTIONS

1. In medium saucepan over medium-low heat, cook cream, cream cheese and rum, stirring often, until cream cheese melts and mixture is hot to touch (do not boil).

2. Remove from heat, add 12 oz chocolate and stir until completely melted. Fold in crushed cookies. Transfer mixture to bowl, cover and refrigerate until firm, at least 2 hr.

3. Line large rimmed baking sheet with parchment paper. Use small spoon to scoop truffle mixture into Tbsp-size balls, carefully rolling between your hands. Place on prepared pan and freeze until very cold and firm, at least 30 min.

4. Melt remaining 12 oz chocolate in microwave. Dip balls in chocolate, tapping off excess, and transfer back to baking sheet. Sprinkle with nutmeg and cinnamon and refrigerate until ready to serve.

Dessert

Flourless Chocolate Walnut Cookies

PER SERVING
~210 cal,
8.5 g fat (2.5 g sat),
3 g pro,
270 mg sodium,
31 g carb, 2 g fiber

These cookies don't need flour to be delicious. They're deeply chocolatey—thanks to cocoa powder and dark chocolate chips—and perfectly balanced with a pinch of flaky salt.

ACTIVE TIME 10 min.   **TOTAL TIME** 30 min.   **YIELDS** 15 servings

INGREDIENTS

- 3 cups confectioners' sugar
- ¾ cup Dutch-processed cocoa powder
- ½ tsp kosher salt
- 2 large eggs, at room temp
- 1 tsp pure vanilla extract
- 1 cup toasted walnuts, chopped
- ½ cup bittersweet or dark chocolate chips
- Flaky sea salt

DIRECTIONS

1. Heat oven to 350°F. Line 2 baking sheets with parchment paper and lightly coat with cooking spray.

2. In medium bowl, whisk together sugar, cocoa powder and salt. In large bowl using electric mixer, beat together eggs and vanilla. Add sugar mixture and mix to combine; fold in walnuts and chocolate chips.

3. Spoon batter (about 1½ Tbsp per cookie) onto prepared baking sheets, spacing 2 in. apart, and sprinkle with flaky sea salt.

4. Bake, rotating positions of pans once, until cookies are puffed and tops begin to crack, 12 to 14 min. Let cool on baking sheets 5 min., then slide parchment and cookies to wire racks to cool completely.

Dessert

Pecan Sticky Buns

This stellar sweet uses store-bought puff pastry so you don't have to deal with any dough. Just dust it with cinnamon, roll and bake in a muffin tin with sugar and pecans until your whole house smells amazing.

PER SERVING
~255 cal,
17 g fat (7.5 g sat),
3 g pro,
140 mg sodium,
30 g carb, 2 g fiber

ACTIVE TIME 15 min. **TOTAL TIME** 35 min. **YIELDS** 12 servings

INGREDIENTS

- ¼ cup (½ stick) cold unsalted butter, cut into 12 slices
- ½ cup firmly packed light brown sugar
- ½ cup pecans, coarsely chopped
- 2 sheets frozen puff pastry, thawed
- 1 tsp ground cinnamon, divided

DIRECTIONS

1. Heat oven to 375°F. Place 1 slice of butter in each cup of 12-cup muffin tin. Top with sugar, then pecans.

2. Unfold one sheet of puff pastry onto cutting board. Gently rub ½ tsp cinnamon onto one side. Cut into 6 strips (each about 1½ in. wide). Work with 1 strip at a time: Hold each end of the strip, loosely twist, then shape into a coil. Tuck end under center and place on top of pecans. Repeat with remaining pastry sheet and cinnamon.

3. Bake until pastry is puffed and golden brown, 20 to 22 min. Remove from oven and immediately invert onto baking sheet. Let cool 5 min. before serving.

Dessert

Meyer Lemon Madeleines

Juice from Meyer lemons adds delicious flavor to these dainty cakes. You can also try them using pink lemons, clementines, Cara Cara oranges or other favorite citrus fruits.

PER SERVING
~110 cal,
6 g fat (2.5 g sat),
1 g pro,
65 mg sodium,
13 g carb, 0 g fiber

ACTIVE TIME 15 min. **TOTAL TIME** 30 min., plus chilling **YIELDS** 18 servings

INGREDIENTS

- 2/3 cup all-purpose flour, plus more for dusting
- 1 tsp baking powder
- 1/4 tsp kosher salt
- 2 large eggs, at room temp
- 1/3 cup granulated sugar
- 1/2 cup (1 stick) unsalted butter, melted, plus more for pan
- 2 tsp grated Meyer lemon zest
- 2 Tbsp whole milk
- 3/4 cup confectioners' sugar
- 1 Tbsp lemon juice

DIRECTIONS

1. In medium bowl, whisk together flour, baking powder and salt.

2. In large bowl, whisk together eggs and granulated sugar until pale and slightly thickened, 2 to 3 min.

3. Gently fold in flour mixture, then fold in melted butter and lemon zest until fully incorporated. Stir in milk (batter should be smooth and shiny). Press piece of plastic wrap against surface of batter, then refrigerate until chilled, at least 1 hr. and up to 2 days.

4. Place rimmed baking sheet in oven and heat oven to 400°F. Brush madeleine pan with melted butter, then dust with flour and tap out excess.

5. Fill madeleine molds 2/3 to 3/4 full (there will be some leftover batter for second batch). Place madeleine pan on preheated baking sheet and bake until golden brown and rounded tops spring back when touched, 11 to 13 min. Remove pan from oven and immediately release madeleines from pan by rapping pan on counter. Transfer to wire rack to cool. Repeat with remaining batter.

6. Meanwhile, prepare icing: In small bowl, whisk together confectioners' sugar, lemon juice and 2 Tbsp water; drizzle over madeleines.

CHAPTER FOUR: DESSERT

Dessert

Pecan Berry Bursts

Dust homemade pecan cookies in a colorful combo of confectioners' sugar and freeze-dried fruit for a low-carb and low-cal dessert.

PER SERVING
~160 cal,
10.5 g fat (5 g sat),
2 g pro,
30 mg sodium,
15 g carb, 1 g fiber

ACTIVE TIME 40 min.   **TOTAL TIME** 55 min., plus chilling   **YIELDS** 2 dozen

INGREDIENTS

- 1 cup pecans (about 3 oz)
- 1¼ cups confectioners' sugar, divided
- 1 cup (2 sticks) unsalted butter, cut into small pieces
- 1 tsp pure vanilla extract
- 2 cups all-purpose flour
- ¼ tsp kosher salt plus more for berry sugars
- ¼ cup freeze-dried strawberries
- ¼ cup freeze-dried raspberries

DIRECTIONS

1. Heat oven to 350°F. Line 2 baking sheets with parchment paper. In food processor, pulse pecans and ¾ cup sugar until pecans are finely ground.

2. Add butter and process until smooth. Mix in vanilla. Add flour and salt and process until combined. Roll dough into 1-in. balls and place on prepared sheets, spacing about 1½ in. apart.

3. Bake, rotating sheets halfway through, until cookies are set and just barely turning light golden brown around edges, 15 to 18 min. Transfer to wire rack.

4. Meanwhile, clean and dry food processor. Process strawberries, ¼ cup sugar and pinch of salt until powdery; transfer to bowl. Repeat with raspberries, remaining ¼ cup sugar and pinch of salt.

5. Just before serving, roll half of cookies in strawberry sugar, dusting them to fully coat. Repeat with remaining cookies and raspberry sugar.

Dessert

Fudgy Beet Brownies

Love 'em or hate 'em, beets are a surprisingly delicious way to amp up a classic brownie recipe and get a dose of veggies, too!

PER SERVING
~160 cal,
11 g fat (6.5 g sat),
3 g pro,
55 mg sodium,
16 g carb, 2 g fiber

ACTIVE TIME 20 min.   **TOTAL TIME** 50 min.   **YIELDS** 16 servings

INGREDIENTS

- ½ cup (1 stick) unsalted butter, plus more for pan
- 6 oz bittersweet chocolate, chopped
- ½ cup firmly packed brown sugar
- 8 oz cooked and peeled whole beets (about 4 small beets), pureed in blender or food processor
- 1 tsp pure vanilla extract
- 1 tsp espresso powder
- ¼ tsp kosher salt
- 2 large eggs, at room temperature
- ½ cup white whole wheat flour

DIRECTIONS

1. Heat oven to 350°F. Butter 8-in. square baking dish and line bottom with parchment paper, leaving overhang on each side. Butter paper.

2. Melt ½ cup butter and chocolate in medium saucepan on low, stirring occasionally, until smooth. Remove from heat, let cool slightly, then whisk in sugar, beets, vanilla, espresso powder and salt. Whisk in eggs one at a time until fully incorporated. Fold in flour until just combined.

3. Pour batter into prepared baking dish and bake until knife inserted in center comes out clean or with just a few moist crumbs attached, 30 to 35 min. Let cool in pan 10 min., then use overhangs to transfer to cutting board. Cut into 16 squares.

Dessert

Italian Shaved Ice Granita

Made with lemonade, limoncello and raspberries, this boozy frozen treat is the ideal light dessert after a hearty Italian meal.

PER SERVING
~95 cal,
0 g fat (0 g sat),
0 g pro,
5 mg sodium,
16 g carb, 1 g fiber

ACTIVE TIME 10 min. **TOTAL TIME** 10 min., plus freezing **YIELDS** 8 servings

INGREDIENTS

- 2 cups lemonade
- ½ cup limoncello
- 6 oz fresh or frozen raspberries
- Zest of 1 lemon
- Raspberries and lemon zest, for topping

DIRECTIONS

1. In blender, puree lemonade, limoncello, raspberries and lemon zest until smooth. Pour into metal loaf or square pan, cover and freeze until set, about 4 hr.

2. To serve, use fork to scrape surface of ice to create large flakes. Divide among bowls. Top with raspberries and zest, if desired.

Dessert

Pumpkin Spice Mousse

This light and creamy pumpkin confection is the ultimate tastes-like-fall treat.

PER SERVING
~195 cal,
14.5 g fat (9 g sat),
3 g pro,
55 mg sodium,
14 g carb, 1 g fiber

ACTIVE TIME 25 min.   **TOTAL TIME** 30 min., plus cooling and chilling   **YIELDS** 16 servings

INGREDIENTS

- 1 **15-oz can pure pumpkin (1¾ cups)**
- 1 **tsp grated peeled fresh ginger**
- ¼ **tsp ground cinnamon**
- ¼ **tsp freshly ground nutmeg**
- **Kosher salt**
- 3 **oz cream cheese, cubed**
- 1 **tsp pure vanilla extract**
- 1 **cup sweetened condensed milk**
- 2 **cups heavy cream, cold**
- **Sour cream and crushed ginger cookies, for serving**

DIRECTIONS

1. In medium saucepan, combine pumpkin, ginger, cinnamon, nutmeg and pinch salt. Cook on medium, stirring frequently, until steaming heavily, darker in color and slightly thicker, about 5 min.

2. Remove from heat and stir in cream cheese and vanilla until smooth. Transfer to bowl, then stir in condensed milk. Let cool completely.

3. Using electric mixer, beat cream until medium peaks form. Fold in cream cheese mixture, then spoon into 4-oz jars. Chill until ready to serve. Serve dolloped with sour cream and crushed ginger cookies if desired.

Dessert

White Chocolate & Lavender Madeleines

PER SERVING
~155 cal,
10 g fat (6 g sat),
2 g pro,
105 mg sodium,
14 g carb, 0 g fiber

White chocolate lovers, this dessert is for you! Sprinkled with relaxing lavender, it's the perfect way to end the day.

ACTIVE TIME 15 min.   **TOTAL TIME** 30 min.   **YIELDS** 12 servings

INGREDIENTS

- 2/3 cup all-purpose flour, plus more for dusting
- 1 tsp baking powder
- 1/4 tsp kosher salt
- 1/2 cup (1 stick) unsalted butter, plus more for pan
- 1 tsp lavender, plus more for decorating
- 2 large eggs, at room temperature
- 1/3 cup sugar
- 2 Tbsp whole milk
- 2 oz white chocolate, chopped

DIRECTIONS

1. In medium bowl, whisk together flour, baking powder and salt. Set aside. In small saucepan, melt butter, then add lavender and let steep 5 min.; strain and set aside.

2. In bowl, whisk together eggs and sugar until pale and slightly thickened, 2 to 3 min.

3. Gently fold in flour mixture, then fold in melted butter until fully incorporated. Stir in milk (batter should be smooth and shiny). Press piece of plastic wrap against surface of batter, then refrigerate until chilled, at least 1 hr. and up to 2 days.

4. Place rimmed baking sheet in oven and heat oven to 400°F. Brush madeleine pan with melted butter, then dust with flour and tap out excess.

5. Evenly divide batter among molds. Place madeleine pan on preheated baking sheet and bake until golden and rounded tops spring back when touched, 11 to 13 min. Remove pan from oven and immediately release madeleines from pan by rapping pan on counter. Let cool on wire rack.

6. Melt chocolate per pkg. directions. Dip half of each madeleine in chocolate, then sprinkle with lavender and let set.

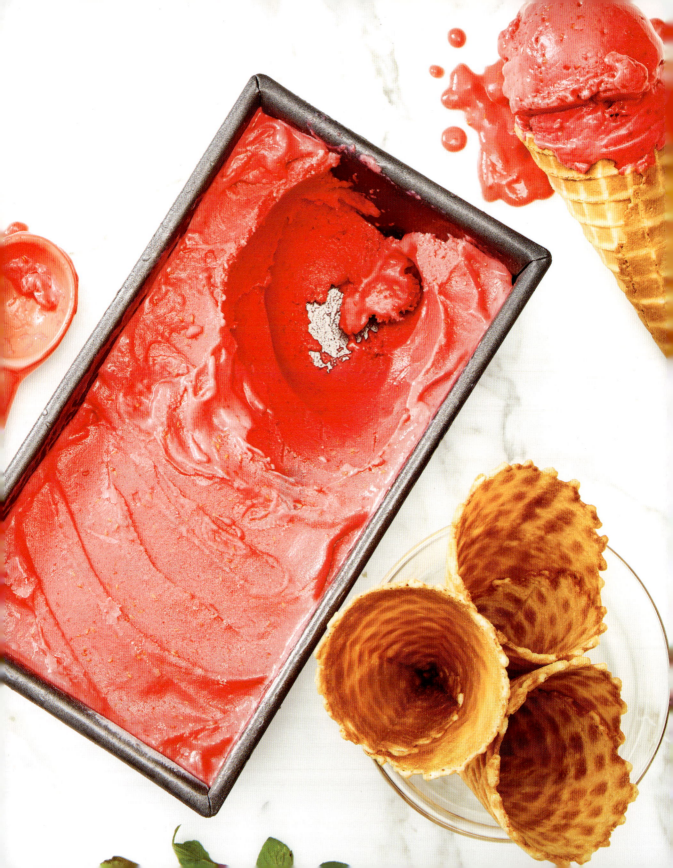

Dessert

No-Churn Mango Berry Ice Cream

Store-bought low-calorie ice cream is often loaded with processed ingredients. This 4-ingredient homemade version is just as satisfying, and it's surprisingly simple to whip up.

PER SERVING
~230 cal.
3.5 g fat (2 g sat),
5 g pro,
290 mg sodium,
51 g carb, 8 g fiber

ACTIVE TIME 15 min.   **TOTAL TIME** 4 hr. 10 min.   **YIELDS** 4 servings

INGREDIENTS

- 1½ lbs frozen raspberries
- ½ lb frozen mango
- ½ cup sweetened condensed milk (7 oz)
- ½ tsp kosher salt

DIRECTIONS

1. In food processor, pulse fruit, scraping side of bowl often, until finely chopped and fluffy.

2. Add sweetened condensed milk and salt and pulse, occasionally scraping side of bowl, until mixture is smooth and whirring around blade in continuous wave.

3. Transfer mixture to 9- by 5-in. loaf pan. Freeze, uncovered, until set, about 4 hr. If not serving immediately, cover tightly with plastic wrap and freeze up to 2 weeks.

Dessert

Vanilla Bean Clafoutis

with Raspberries & Nectarines

Save your arm the trouble of whisking and use your blender to quickly make the light batter for this summery fruit tart.

PER SERVING
~265 cal,
10.5 g fat (5.5 g sat),
7 g pro,
175 mg sodium,
38 g carb, 3 g fiber

ACTIVE TIME 20 min. **TOTAL TIME** 1 hr. 5 min. **YIELDS** 8 servings

INGREDIENTS

- 1 **Tbsp unsalted butter, at room temperature, for greasing**
- ½ **cup plus 1 Tbsp granulated sugar, divided, plus more for pan**
- 1 **lemon, zested and juiced**
- 1½ **lb nectarines, pitted and cut into ½-in.-thick wedges**
- 6 **oz raspberries**
- 1 **vanilla bean**
- 4 **large eggs**
- 1 **cup whole milk**
- ¾ **cup all-purpose flour, sifted**
- ½ **cup heavy cream**
- ½ **tsp kosher salt**
- **Confectioners' sugar, for dusting**

DIRECTIONS

1. Heat oven to 350°F. Grease 2½-qt baking dish with butter and lightly dust with granulated sugar.

2. In medium bowl, place 2 tsp lemon zest, then add 1 Tbsp lemon juice. Add nectarines, raspberries and 1 Tbsp granulated sugar and gently toss to combine.

3. Cut vanilla bean in half lengthwise and scrape out seeds and pulp. In blender, combine eggs, milk, flour, cream, salt, remaining ½ cup granulated sugar, and vanilla seeds and pulp (discard pod). Blend on high until slightly frothy, about 1 min.

4. Transfer fruit to prepared dish along with any juices and pour batter on top. Bake until just set, 45 to 50 min. Let cool 5 min. before serving. Dust with confectioners' sugar if desired.

CHAPTER FOUR: DESSERT

Dessert

Clementine Honey Granita

This granita hits the spot as a palate cleanser or light dessert. If you have leftovers, try adding a scoop to a glass of prosecco for a fun cocktail.

PER SERVING
~96 cal,
0 g fat (0 g sat),
1 g pro,
28 mg sodium,
25 g carb, 0 g fiber

ACTIVE TIME 10 min. **TOTAL TIME** 3 hr. 10 min. **YIELDS** 4-6 servings

INGREDIENTS

- ¼ cup honey
- 1 Tbsp grated clementine zest
- Kosher salt
- 2 cups freshly squeezed clementine or tangerine juice (from about 16 clementines or 8 tangerines)
- 2 Tbsp fresh lemon juice
- Sparkling water

DIRECTIONS

1. In small saucepan, bring ¼ cup water and honey to boil. Remove from heat and stir in grated clementine zest and pinch of salt; let sit 5 min.

2. Whisk in clementine or tangerine juice and lemon juice. Transfer to 8- by 8-in. metal pan and freeze until firm, 3 to 4 hr. Using fork, scrape up flakes and transfer to glasses. Serve topped with sparkling water.

Yellow Split Pea Dip
p. 303

Muhammara Dip
p. 301

Chapter Five
Snacks

Spinach & Yogurt Dip
p. 299

Snacks

Dill Dip

Refreshing, herbal and perfectly creamy, this dip will transport you directly to Greece. Enjoy scoops of it with veggies or bread, or use it as a spread to give a turkey burger a little more pizzazz.

1 TBSP SERVING
~15 cal,
0.5 g fat (0.5 g sat),
1 g pro,
30 mg sodium,
1 g carb, 0 g fiber

ACTIVE TIME 10 min.   **TOTAL TIME** 10 min.   **YIELDS** 2½ cups

INGREDIENTS

- 2 cups plain Greek yogurt
- 2 tsp grated lemon zest
- 1 Tbsp lemon juice
- Kosher salt and pepper
- 2 scallions, finely chopped
- ¼ cup flat-leaf parsley, chopped
- ¼ cup fresh dill, roughly chopped, plus more for topping
- Cut vegetables, crackers and bread, for serving

DIRECTIONS

1. In bowl, combine yogurt, lemon zest and juice and ½ tsp each salt and pepper. Fold in scallion, parsley and dill.

2. Serve topped with more dill and cracked pepper, and with veggies, crackers and bread for dipping.

Snacks

Chickpea "Nuts"

Next time a snack attack hits, make a batch of these crunchy, crispy chickpeas—one serving has just 110 calories.

¼ CUP SERVING
~110 cal,
5 g fat (0.5 g sat),
4 g pro,
240 mg sodium,
13 g carb, 4 g fiber

ACTIVE TIME 5 min.   **TOTAL TIME** 5 min.   **YIELDS** 2 cups

INGREDIENTS

- 2 **15-oz cans chickpeas**
- 2 Tbsp **extra virgin olive oil**
- ¼ tsp **salt**
- ¼ tsp **pepper**

DIRECTIONS

1. Heat oven to 425°F. Rinse and drain chickpeas; pat very dry with paper towels, discarding any loose skins. On large rimmed baking sheet, toss with olive oil, salt and pepper. Roast for 30 min. until crisp, shaking occasionally. Remove from oven and transfer to bowl; toss with seasonings if desired. Chickpeas will continue to crisp as they cool.

FUN FLAVORS

Honey-Sesame
Follow Original Recipe instructions, then toss roasted chickpeas with 2 Tbsp **honey**, 1 Tbsp **sesame oil**, 1 Tbsp **sesame seeds**, 1 Tbsp **sugar**, ½ tsp **garlic powder** and ½ tsp **five-spice powder**. Return to oven for 5 min. until caramelized and crisp.

BBQ
Follow Original Recipe instructions, then toss roasted chickpeas in 1 tsp **dark brown sugar**, ½ tsp **ground cumin**, ½ tsp **ground paprika**, ½ tsp **garlic powder** and ½ tsp **chili powder**. Return to oven for 5 min. until dry and crisp.

Masala
Follow Original Recipe instructions, then toss roasted chickpeas in ½ tsp **garam masala**, ½ tsp **ground cumin**, ½ tsp **ground ginger** and ¼ tsp **cayenne**. Return to oven for 5 min. until dry and crisp.

Spicy Buffalo
Follow Original Recipe instructions, then toss roasted chickpeas in ¼ cup **cayenne pepper hot sauce**. Return to oven for 5 min. until dry and crisp.

Maple Cinnamon
Follow Original Recipe instructions, then toss roasted chickpeas in 2 Tbsp **maple syrup**, 2 tsp **sugar**, 1 tsp **ground cinnamon** and ¼ tsp **ground nutmeg**. Return to oven for 5 min. until caramelized and crisp.

Parmesan-Herb
Follow Original Recipe instructions, then toss roasted chickpeas in ¼ cup **Parmesan cheese**, finely grated, 1 tsp **garlic powder**, 1 tsp **fresh rosemary**, finely chopped and 1 tsp loosely packed **lemon zest**.

Snacks

Roasted Strawberries & Brie

Low on effort yet big on impact, this snack will satisfy sweet and salty cravings. It works well as an appetizer, snack or even a dessert.

PER ¼ CUP SERVING
~205 cal,
13 g fat (8 g sat),
10 g pro,
310 mg sodium,
14 g carb, 2 g fiber

ACTIVE TIME 5 min. **TOTAL TIME** 15 min. **YIELDS** 4–6 servings

INGREDIENTS

- Roasted Strawberries (recipe below)
- 1 8-oz wheel Brie cheese
- Fresh thyme
- Bread and crackers, for serving

DIRECTIONS

1. Heat oven to 350°F. Prepare strawberries. Eight min. before strawberries are finished, line large baking sheet with parchment and place Brie on top, or place Brie in small cast-iron skillet. Bake 7 min.

2. Transfer to platter if not in cast-iron skillet, then spoon some roasted strawberries on top. Sprinkle with thyme and serve with bread and crackers if desired. Serve with remaining strawberries.

ROASTED STRAWBERRIES

Heat oven to 350°F. Line 9- by 13-in. baking pan with parchment, leaving 1-in. overhang on 2 long sides. In prepared pan, toss 1 lb halved **strawberries** with 2 Tbsp warmed **honey** and pinch of **salt**. Scrape ½ **vanilla bean** and toss seeds and pod with strawberry mixture. Roast, stirring once, until strawberries are tender and juices start to reduce but not brown, 40 to 50 min.

Snacks

Spinach & Yogurt Dip

This dip relies heavily on kitchen staples, like frozen spinach and Greek yogurt. Keep them on hand so you're always prepared to whip up this tangy snack at a moment's notice.

PER 4 TBSP SERVING
~120 cal,
8.5 g fat (2 g sat),
7 g pro,
165 mg sodium,
5 g carb, 1 g fiber

ACTIVE TIME 25 min.   **TOTAL TIME** 25 min.   **YIELDS** 2 2/3 cups

INGREDIENTS

- 3 Tbsp olive oil, divided
- 1 small onion, finely chopped
- 1 large clove garlic, finely chopped
- 8 oz frozen leaf spinach, thawed and squeezed dry
- 2 cups plain Greek yogurt
- 1 Tbsp fresh lemon juice
- Kosher salt and pepper
- 1/4 cup fresh mint leaves, coarsely chopped

DIRECTIONS

1. Heat 1 Tbsp oil in large skillet on medium. Add onion and cook, stirring occasionally, until tender, 5 to 6 min. Stir in garlic and cook 2 min.; transfer to bowl.

2. Chop spinach and toss with onion mixture. Fold in yogurt, lemon juice and 1/2 tsp each salt and pepper.

3. Heat remaining 2 Tbsp oil in medium skillet until shimmering. Add mint and cook until sizzling and fragrant, 1 min. Let cool slightly, then spoon over yogurt dip.

Snacks

Muhammara Dip

PER 4 TBSP SERVING
~100 cal,
8.5 g fat (1 g sat),
2 g pro,
135 mg sodium,
6 g carb, 1 g fiber

This flavorful Middle Eastern dip is normally served with pita bread but would go just as well with cut-up veggies.

ACTIVE TIME 10 min. **TOTAL TIME** 35 min. **YIELDS** 2¾ cups

INGREDIENTS

- 3 red peppers, halved and seeded
- 2 Tbsp olive oil, divided, plus more for topping
- ½ cup walnuts, plus more for topping
- 1 Tbsp fresh lemon juice
- 1 clove garlic, finely chopped
- ½ tsp ground sumac
- ¼ tsp cayenne
- Kosher salt
- ⅓ cup fresh breadcrumbs
- Pomegranate molasses (optional)

DIRECTIONS

1. Rub peppers with 1 Tbsp oil and place, cut side down, on foil-lined baking sheet. Broil until skin starts to blacken, 8 to 10 min. Immediately transfer to bowl; cover with plastic wrap and let sit until tender, 12 min. Remove and discard skin.

2. In food processor, pulse walnuts, lemon juice, garlic, sumac, cayenne, remaining Tbsp of olive oil and ½ tsp salt to combine. Pulse in peppers until mostly smooth but still a bit chunky. Stir in breadcrumbs.

3. Transfer to serving bowl. Drizzle with oil and pomegranate molasses, if using, and sprinkle with more walnuts.

Snacks

Yellow Split Pea Dip

As eye-catching as it is appetizing, this high-fiber dip contains anti-inflammatory turmeric to boost your immune system.

PER 4 TBSP SERVING
~130 cal,
4.5 g fat (0.5 g sat),
6 g pro,
120 mg sodium,
18 g carb, 7 g fiber

ACTIVE TIME 10 min. **TOTAL TIME** 1 hr. 10 min. **YIELDS** 2½ cups

INGREDIENTS

- 1 cup yellow split peas
- 1 small onion, finely chopped
- 1 large clove garlic, pressed
- 1 bay leaf
- ½ tsp ground turmeric
- Kosher salt
- 2 Tbsp olive oil, plus more for topping
- 1 Tbsp fresh lemon juice
- Finely chopped red onion, finely chopped parsley and paprika, for topping

DIRECTIONS

1. In small saucepan, combine split peas with 2½ cups water and bring to boil, skimming foam that rises to surface. Lower heat and add onion, garlic, bay leaf, turmeric and ½ tsp salt and simmer until split peas are very tender, 50 to 60 min.

2. Discard bay leaf and transfer split pea mixture, including any liquid, to food processor. Add olive oil and lemon juice and puree until smooth.

3. Transfer to serving bowl, drizzle with additional olive oil and top with red onion, parsley and sprinkle of paprika if desired.

Snacks

Fried Plantains

Just two ingredients are all you need to create this popular South American treat. Enjoy it as a snack or add it to almost any dish as a decadent side.

PER 4 TBSP SERVING
~135 cal,
9.5 g fat (1 g sat),
1 g pro,
120 mg sodium,
14 g carb, 1 g fiber

ACTIVE TIME 10 min. **TOTAL TIME** 20 min. **YIELDS** 8 servings

INGREDIENTS

- Canola oil, for frying
- 2 very ripe plantains (skin should be very black and soft)
- Kosher salt

DIRECTIONS

1. Heat ¼ in. oil (about 1½ cups) in large, heavy skillet on medium.

2. Peel plantains by cutting off ends and making long, shallow cut lengthwise through peel. Slice at angle into ½-in.-thick pieces.

3. Reduce heat to medium-low and, in 2 batches, fry plantains until golden brown and caramelized, 3 to 6 min. per side. Transfer to paper-towel-lined plate to drain. Sprinkle with ½ tsp salt.

Snacks

Spring Crudités

with Herbed Cheese Dip

There's no better accompaniment to a rainbow of veggies. This tangy and fresh-tasting dip will be ready and on the table in 10 minutes flat.

PER SERVING
~105 cal,
8 g fat (5.5 g sat),
7 g pro,
265 mg sodium,
2 g carb, 0 g fiber

ACTIVE TIME 10 min. **TOTAL TIME** 10 min. **YIELDS** 8 servings

INGREDIENTS

- 8 oz fresh goat cheese, at room temperature
- ½ cup ricotta cheese
- 1 scallion, finely chopped
- ½ small clove garlic, finely grated
- ¼ cup fresh flat-leaf parsley, chopped, plus more for topping
- ¼ cup fresh mint, chopped
- 2 Tbsp fresh chives, chopped, plus more for topping
- 2 tsp finely grated lemon zest
- 2 Tbsp lemon juice (from 2 lemons)
- Kosher salt and pepper
- Cut vegetables, for serving (we used radishes, carrots, endive, snap peas and seedless cucumber)

DIRECTIONS

1. In food processor, pulse goat cheese and ricotta until smooth.

2. Transfer to bowl and fold in scallion and garlic. Fold in parsley, mint, chives, lemon zest and juice and ½ tsp each salt and pepper.

3. Spoon into serving bowl and sprinkle with more parsley and chives if desired. Serve with cut vegetables.

CHAPTER FIVE: SNACKS

Snacks

Zesty Beet Dip

Loaded with antioxidants, this pretty pink dip has a crunchy texture and a zesty bite from horseradish. And it's low-carb and low in calories, too! Snack on it with veggies or spread it on your favorite sandwich.

PER 4 TBSP SERVING
~115 cal, 8.5 g fat (1 g sat), 3 g pro, 280 mg sodium, 8 g carb, 2 g fiber

ACTIVE TIME 5 min.   **TOTAL TIME** 5 min.   **YIELDS** 5 servings

INGREDIENTS

- 8 oz cooked beets (about 5 small beets)
- 1/3 cup walnuts, toasted
- 1/4 cup prepared horseradish, squeezed of excess moisture
- 1/4 cup plain Greek yogurt
- 1 Tbsp fresh lemon juice
- 1 Tbsp olive oil
- Kosher salt and pepper

DIRECTIONS

1. In blender on low to medium speed, puree beets, walnuts, horseradish, yogurt, lemon juice, olive oil, ½ tsp salt and ¼ tsp pepper until very smooth.

Snacks

Best Ever Spinach Artichoke Dip

A healthy take on the timeless spinach-artichoke dip, this lighter version gets its creaminess from cannellini beans and a bit of Parmesan.

PER ¼ CUP SERVING
~55 cal,
1 g fat (0.5 g sat),
3.5 g pro,
195 mg sodium,
7 g carb, 2 g fiber

ACTIVE TIME 5 min.   **TOTAL TIME** 5 min.   **YIELDS** 1¾ cups

INGREDIENTS

- 1 14-oz can artichoke hearts, rinsed, squeezed of excess moisture and patted dry
- 1 cup packed baby spinach
- ½ cup cannellini beans, rinsed
- 1 scallion, chopped
- Finely grated zest of 1 lemon (about 1 Tbsp)
- 2 Tbsp lemon juice
- 1 oz Parmesan cheese, finely grated
- Pepper

DIRECTIONS

1. In blender, puree artichoke hearts, spinach, beans, scallion, lemon zest and juice, Parmesan and ½ tsp pepper until finely chopped.

Snacks

Zucchanoush

For a fun, summery twist on baba ganoush, try swapping out eggplants for zucchini to take advantage of the summer squash in its peak season.

PER ¼ CUP SERVING
~125 cal,
11.5 g fat (1.5 g sat),
3 g pro,
145 mg sodium,
4.5 g carb, 1 g fiber

ACTIVE TIME 15 min.   **TOTAL TIME** 15 min.   **YIELDS** 7 servings

INGREDIENTS

- 1 lb small zucchini (about 3), quartered lengthwise
- 3 Tbsp olive oil, divided
- Kosher salt and pepper
- 1 clove garlic
- ¼ cup tahini *or cream cheese*
- 2 Tbsp fresh lemon juice
- 3 Tbsp mint leaves, divided
- 1 Tbsp pine nuts, toasted

DIRECTIONS

1. Heat grill to medium. Toss zucchini with 1 Tbsp oil and ½ tsp salt and grill until tender and evenly charred, 8 to 10 min.

2. Transfer zucchini to blender along with garlic, tahini, lemon juice and 1 Tbsp mint and pulse to combine. With motor running on low speed, drizzle in remaining 2 Tbsp olive oil and puree until mostly smooth, increasing blender speed if necessary.

3. Chop remaining mint. Serve zucchini mixture topped with mint and pine nuts.

Snacks

Charred Salsa

Taco Tuesday will never be the same with this smoky salsa. This two-step recipe will be just as delicious if you use a grill pan.

PER ¼ CUP SERVING
~10 cal,
0 g fat (0 g sat),
0 g pro,
80 mg sodium,
2 g carb, 1 g fiber

ACTIVE TIME 15 min. **TOTAL TIME** 20 min. **YIELDS** 12 servings

INGREDIENTS

- 1 lb tomatoes, halved if large
- 1 small onion (skin on), halved
- 1 small garlic clove, skin on
- 1 jalapeño
- ¼ cup cilantro
- Kosher salt

DIRECTIONS

1. Heat grill to medium-high. Grill tomatoes, onion, garlic and jalapeño, turning occasionally, until charred on all sides, about 10 min. total. Let cool 10 min.

2. Remove skins from onion and garlic and transfer all vegetables to blender. Add cilantro and ½ tsp salt and puree until mostly smooth.

Snacks

Prosciutto Scallion Bundles

These low-carb bites are total flavor bombs. They take just minutes to cook up, perfect for when you're short on time.

PER SERVING
~60 cal,
4.5 g fat (1 g sat),
3 g pro,
230 mg sodium,
3 g carb, 1 g fiber

ACTIVE TIME 20 min.   **TOTAL TIME** 20 min.   **YIELDS** 8 servings

INGREDIENTS

- 24 scallions, trimmed
- Kosher salt and pepper
- 4 thin slices prosciutto, halved lengthwise
- 2 Tbsp olive oil

DIRECTIONS

1. Season scallions with ¼ tsp each salt and pepper. Wrap 1 piece prosciutto around 3 scallions (white and light green parts), pressing lightly to adhere. Repeat with remaining prosciutto and scallions to make 8 bundles.

2. Heat oil in large skillet on medium-high. Working in 2 batches, cook scallion bundles, turning occasionally, until browned and crisp on all sides, 3 to 4 min., adding more oil to skillet as necessary. Transfer to paper towels, then to platter to serve.

Snacks

Roasted Artichokes
with Caesar Dip

Roasted artichokes serve as the perfect dipper for this cheesy, mustardy sauce.

PER SERVING
~135 cal, 10.5 g fat (2 g sat), 4 g pro, 410 mg sodium, 9 g carb, 4 g fiber

ACTIVE TIME 45 min. **TOTAL TIME** 1 hr. 20 min. **YIELDS** 6 servings

INGREDIENTS

- 3 globe artichokes
- 2 lemons
- 4 Tbsp olive oil
- Kosher salt
- 1 small clove garlic, pressed
- 1 tsp Dijon mustard
- ½ tsp Worcestershire sauce
- ¼ cup grated Parmesan cheese

Good and easy Aug. 2022

DIRECTIONS

1. Heat oven to 425°F and line rimmed baking sheet with foil.

2. Rinse and dry artichokes with paper towel. Trim stems and cut ¼ in. off each top. Use kitchen shears to cut off tip of each leaf. Use hands to pull and loosen leaves to open up artichokes. Slice artichokes in half vertically and use small knife to cut out fuzzy centers and purple leaves.

3. Place artichoke halves on baking sheet, squeeze juice of half of 1 lemon on cut sides and rub lemon half over each. Drizzle with 1 Tbsp olive oil and season with ¼ tsp salt. Flip artichokes and repeat with other lemon half, 1 Tbsp olive oil and ¼ tsp salt.

4. Arrange artichokes cut sides down, cover with foil and roast until golden brown and tender, 35 to 40 min.

5. Meanwhile, sprinkle ¼ tsp salt over garlic; using large knife, rub and scrape salt into garlic to make paste. Transfer to bowl.

6. Finely grate zest of remaining lemon into bowl, then squeeze in juice (you should have at least 3 Tbsp). Whisk in mustard, Worcestershire sauce and remaining 2 Tbsp oil. Stir in Parmesan. Serve with artichokes for dipping.

Snacks

Garlicky Roasted-Radish Bruschetta

PER SERVING
~225 cal,
11.5 g fat (1.5 g sat),
5 g pro,
540 mg sodium,
26 g carb, 4 g fiber

Roasting radishes reduces their bite and gives them a slightly sweet taste, making them the perfect low-cal, nutrient-dense sub for potatoes. Combine them with garlic and serve with a hearty country bread for the ultimate bruschetta.

ACTIVE TIME 15 min. **TOTAL TIME** 25 min. **YIELDS** 4 servings

INGREDIENTS

- 3 Tbsp olive oil, divided
- 1½ lbs small to medium radishes, mixed colors, trimmed and halved (quartered if large), leaves reserved
- 3 cloves garlic (2 thinly sliced)
- 4 slices country bread
- 2 Tbsp chopped flat-leaf parsley
- Kosher salt and pepper

DIRECTIONS

1. Heat oven to 450°F. Coat rimmed baking sheet with 1 Tbsp oil, then add radishes, cut sides down, and drizzle with 1 Tbsp oil. Roast 8 min. Scatter sliced garlic over radishes, rotate baking sheet and roast until bottoms of radishes are golden brown, 6 to 8 min. more.

2. While radishes are roasting, brush bread with remaining Tbsp oil; add to oven along with radishes and toast until golden brown and crisp. Remove from oven and rub with remaining clove garlic.

3. When radishes are done, toss with parsley and ½ tsp each salt and pepper, then fold in 2 cups reserved radish leaves. Spoon over garlic toasts and cut into pieces.

Snacks

Spinach Artichoke Tartines

PER SERVING
~200 cal,
7 g fat (3 g sat),
9 g pro,
655 mg sodium,
26 g carb, 2 g fiber

A little bit of cream cheese goes a long way in this crowd-pleasing toast. The result is a creamy and bright spread that can easily be served as a dip with toast or crudités.

ACTIVE TIME 10 min. **TOTAL TIME** 15 min. **YIELDS** 4 servings

INGREDIENTS

- 2 Tbsp cream cheese, at room temperature
- 1 14.5-oz can artichokes, rinsed and chopped
- 2 cups baby spinach
- ½ cup finely grated Parmesan cheese, divided
- ¼ tsp red pepper flakes
- 4 slices country-style bread

DIRECTIONS

1. Heat broiler. In large bowl, combine cream cheese, artichokes, baby spinach, ¼ cup Parmesan cheese and red pepper flakes.

2. Lightly toast bread, then spread with topping. Sprinkle with remaining Parmesan cheese and broil until golden brown and bubbly, 2 to 3 min.

Snacks

Raspberry Popcorn

Use freeze-dried raspberries to make this easy recipe all year round. One cup of this sweet, salty treat is only 75 calories, making it one to eat by the handful.

PER 1 CUP SERVING
~75 cal,
3 g fat (0 g sat),
2 g pro,
40 mg sodium,
11 g carb, 3 g fiber

ACTIVE TIME 5 min.   **TOTAL TIME** 5 min.   **YIELDS** 6 cups

INGREDIENTS

- ½ cup freeze-dried raspberries
- 2 cups plain popcorn
- ⅛ tsp salt

DIRECTIONS

1. In food processor, pulse freeze-dried raspberries to form a powder.
2. Toss popcorn with canola oil, raspberry powder and salt to coat.

Snacks

Sweet & Salty Maple Popcorn

Sweet, spicy, salty and crunchy, this popcorn satisfies all cravings.

PER ½ CUP SERVING
~160 cal,
12 g fat (1.5 g sat),
6 g pro,
80 mg sodium,
10 g carb, 3 g fiber

ACTIVE TIME 5 min.   **TOTAL TIME** 25 min.   **YIELDS** 6 cups

INGREDIENTS

- 1 cup almonds
- 1 cup peanuts
- 2 Tbsp maple syrup
- ¼ tsp cayenne
- Kosher salt and pepper
- 4 cups plain air-popped popcorn

DIRECTIONS

1. Heat oven to 350°F. In bowl, toss almonds and peanuts with maple syrup, cayenne and ½ tsp each salt and pepper.

2. Transfer to parchment-lined rimmed baking sheet and roast, tossing twice, until nuts are golden brown and caramelized, 20 to 25 min. Let cool slightly, then toss with popcorn.

Thank you for purchasing
Low-Calorie, Big-Flavor

Visit our online store to find more great products from Good Housekeeping and save 20% off your next purchase.

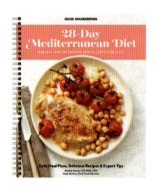  

PLEASE ENJOY 20% OFF AT OUR STORE!

20% OFF

USE COUPON CODE THANKYOU20

SHOP.GOODHOUSEKEEPING.COM

*Exclusions Apply

HEARST